INQUIRY SCIENCE

Grades K–1

Published by
Frank Schaffer Publications®

Editor: Karen Thompson

Frank Schaffer Publications®

Send all inquiries to:
Frank Schaffer Publications
3195 Wilson Drive NW
Grand Rapids, Michigan 49534

Inquiry Science—grades K-1

ISBN 0-7682-3370-4

2 3 4 5 6 7 8 9 MAZ 10 09 08 07

Table of Contents

Table of Contents

Sink and Float

0-7682-3370-4 *Inquiry Science*

Water Wonders

Gearing Up

Engage students by giving them a challenge. Tell them that there is a special liquid substance we use every day. If they can figure out what it is you will let them paint it. Students may ask yes or no questions. When students have guessed the substance is water, let them paint the sidewalks with water.

Have students express what they know about water by contributing words to a water word bank. The word bank should be posted in the classroom and added to throughout the lessons.

> *Process Skills Used*
> • observing
> • investigating
> • communicating

Guided Discovery

Background information for the teacher:
Water has many properties: it has surface tension, it flows, it changes shape to fit any container, it evaporates, and it dissolves some substances.

Materials needed for each group:
water in dishtub
rubber tubing
strainers
food coloring
jars
various containers
measuring cups

Directions for the activity:

Pour water into each tub. Have students observe the water by feeling, smelling, and moving it. Give students numerous containers, strainers, cups, tubing and jars. Direct student explorations by asking the following questions about water:

1. How can you move water from one container to another?
2. What shape is the water?
3. How does the water move?
4. What do you observe about the water?

Responding to Discovery

Discuss the following questions with the class:

• How does water feel, taste, or smell?
• Why is water important?
• When do you use water?
• How do you move the water?
• What color is water?

Have students make water pictures. They will use a damp sponge to lightly *wash* the paper. They will then drip food coloring on the page. When the papers have dried, each student may write a sentence telling something about water.

Applications and Extensions

Have students fill two clear jars halfway with water. Put a lid on one jar and mark the water level on both jars. Place the jars on a sunny windowsill. Watch and record what happens over a week.

> *Real-World Applications*
> • Discuss the importance of drinking water.
> • Discuss the need for water conservation.

0-7682-3370-4 *Inquiry Science*

Water Wonders

🦆 Draw how you used each container and water tool.

🦆 Draw how you moved the water.

🦆 What shape is the water?

_____

_____

🦆 What did you observe about water?

_____

_____

_____

_____

0-7682-3370-4 *Inquiry Science*

Sink or Float

Gearing Up

Hold an orange over a clear bowl of water and ask the students to predict whether it will float or sink. Place the orange in the water and note that it floats. Peel the orange and repeat. Challenge the students to propose why that happened. Brainstorm a list of items that float.

Process Skills Used

- classifying
- observing
- predicting
- communicating

Guided Discovery

Background information for the teacher:
When an object floats, it will rest on the surface of or be suspended in a body of liquid. Buoyancy is the tendency of a body to float or rise when placed in a liquid. When an object sinks, it will fall to the bottom of a body of liquid.

Materials needed for each group:
clear tub
water
paper towels
any 10 items for testing:

paper clip	coin	cork
clay	stone	plastic spoon
marble	ivory soap	whiffle ball
tennis ball	ping pong ball	etc.

Directions for the activity:
Have groups arrange the 10 items into two groups: items they predict will sink and items they predict will float. Each student should record predictions on the activity sheet. Students will work in groups to test the predictions. Students should record their findings on the activity sheet. Groups will sort items into sink and float categories.

Responding to Discovery

Play "Walk, Freeze, Talk" to share what students learned about sinking and floating. Students walk randomly around the room. When the teacher announces "freeze," all students stop and find a partner. The teacher poses one of the following questions for partners to discuss.

- Which objects did you think would float? Sink?
- Why do you think some items floated?
- What items fooled you?
- Which object sank the fastest? Why?
- Did all the objects that floated, float on the top of the water?

Applications and Extensions

- Sing "I am Floating" (to tune of "Frere-Jacques").

  I am floating, I am floating,

  Can it be? Can it be?

  Resting on the water, resting on the water.

  Look and see, look and see.

- Students can bring in items from home to test at a sink/float center.

Real-World Applications

- Design or describe some great bathtub toys.
- What items do people use in their pools?

0-7682-3370-4 *Inquiry Science*

Name _____

Sink or Float

Sink or Float Predictions

❧ Draw or write your predictions.

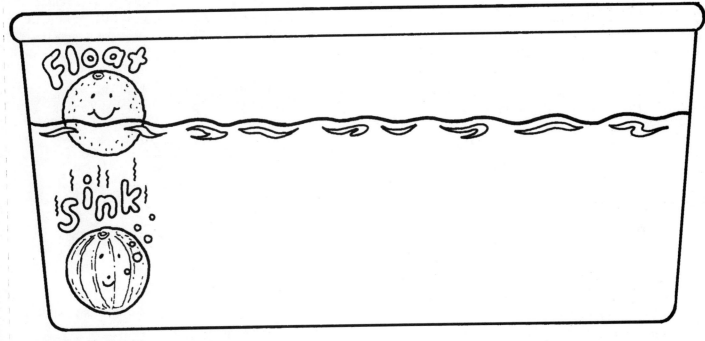

Sink or Float Findings

❧ Draw or write your findings.

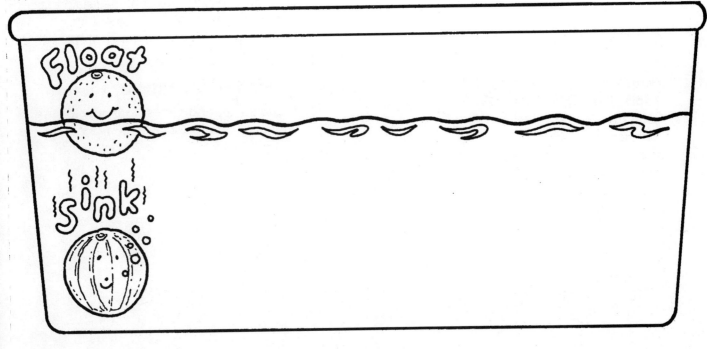

0-7682-3370-4 *Inquiry Science*

Sinking Floaters

Gearing Up

Share the following poem with students:

Two friends went for a sail one day
In a boat out in the bay.
They had some fun and they did play,
Until the storm blew their way.

The boat it rocked and it did sway,
That storm was raging on that day.

Two friends went for a sail one day,
They had some fun and they did play.
Until a storm blew their way,
and sank the boat out in the bay.

Have students discuss and make a list of some reasons a boat might sink.

> ### Process Skills Used
> - sorting
> - investigating
> - communicating

Guided Discovery

Materials for each group:
Items from the "Sink or Float" activity
water
washers
paper clips
clear plastic tub
pennies
tape
marbles
nuts/bolts

Directions for the activity:

As a whole class, select one item that floated from the "Sink or Float" activity. Have students give suggestions on how to sink the item. Test the different suggestions until the item sinks in the water. Break into groups. Assign each group an item that floated in the "Sink or Float" activity. Challenge groups to find a way to sink their items.

Responding to Discovery

Have groups share their solutions to sinking the item.

Create a bulletin board.

The bulletin board will have a water line. Each student draws the item that he or she sank and completes a sentence strip to go with the picture: "A _____ might sink." Student pictures and sentence strips will go below the waterline.

Applications and Extensions

Students continue to explore how to sink "floating" items at a classroom center.

> ### Real-World Applications
> - What is in a life preserver that makes it float?

Published by Frank Schaffer Publications. Copyright protected.
0-7682-3370-4 *Inquiry Science*

Name _____

Sinking Floaters

First the _____ floated.

The _____ sank when _____

_____ .

✎ Draw what you did to make the floater sink.

0-7682-3370-4 *Inquiry Science*

Floating Sinkers

Gearing Up

Before students arrive, sink an empty bottle to the bottom of a clear tank of water. Ask the students to suggest ways to make the bottle float. Demonstrate how to raise the bottle by placing a piece of tubing into the bottle and blowing into it until the bottle floats.

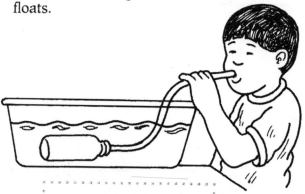

Process Skills Used
- predicting
- communicating
- investigating

Guided Discovery

Background information for the teacher:
An object's ability to float on water depends on the amount of water it displaces.

Materials needed for each group:
dishtub of water
rubber tubing
objects from "Sink or Float" activity
various floating materials such as craft sticks, straws, toothpicks, balloons, Styrofoam, etc.

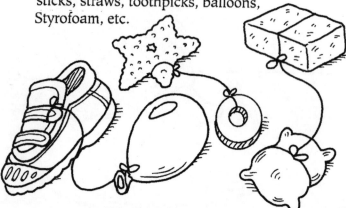

Directions for the activity:

As a whole class, select one item that sank from the "Sink or Float" activity. Have students give suggestions on how to make the item float. Test the different suggestions until the item floats in the water. Break into groups. Assign each group an item that sank in the "Sink or Float" activity. Challenge groups to find a way to float the item.

Responding to Discovery

Have groups share their solutions to floating the items.

Students will add items to the bulletin board. This time they draw the items that they floated. Each student should complete a sentence strip that says, "A _____ will float."

Applications and Extensions

Students continue to investigate how to float "sinking" items at a classroom center.

Real-World Applications
- Why do you think a steel ship floats?
- Have you tried floating items while playing in the tub?

0-7682-3370-4 *Inquiry Science*

Name _____

Floating Sinkers

First the _____ sank.

The _____ floated when _____

_____ .

🐌 Draw what you did to make the sinker float.

0-7682-3370-4 *Inquiry Science*

Shapes That Float

Gearing Up

Cut out (or have students find and cut out) pictures of various boats from magazines. Ask the students to sort and graph the boats in meaningful categories. Challenge students to examine the different shapes and kinds of boats to get ideas for their own "floating creations."

> *Process Skills Used*
> - graphing
> - observing
> - classifying

Guided Discovery

Materials needed for each group:
craft sticks
cardboard
scissors
wood
sponges
straws
corks
Styrofoam trays or pieces
dishtub of water
paper towels
toy boats
3" x 5" cards

Directions for the activity:
Discuss which shape will make the best floating boat. Each student or pair of students constructs a boat that will float well in the water. Students test their boats in the water.

Responding to Discovery

Play a classification game.

Each student stands and describes his or her boat in a sentence. Other students may stand if the description fits their boats. Hold a discussion with students about how the boats are the same and different.

Have students name their boats. Display the boats with name cards in the classroom.

Applications and Extensions

Sing "Float Your Boat"
(to the tune of "Row, Row, Row Your Boat")

> Float, float, float your boat
> Gently on the water.
> Slowly moving, slowly moving,
> Boating is a dream.

Students may create new verses about their boats for the song.

> *Real-World Applications*
> - Are all boats shaped the same?

0-7682-3370-4 *Inquiry Science*

Shapes That Float

🐦 Draw your plan for your floating boat.

🐦 Test your boat. Make changes if it doesn't float.
Draw your completed boat in the water.

🐦 Push your boat. Describe how it moves in the water.

_____

_____

_____

_____

0-7682-3370-4 *Inquiry Science*

Floating and Sinking Substances

Gearing Up

Pour different liquids (milk, oil, soda pop, corn syrup, and water) in baby food jars. Allow the students to handle the sealed jars. Have the students make observations and compare the different liquids. Compare the movement of each liquid to the jar of water. Tell students that today we're going to find out if items sink or float in these liquids.

> *Process Skills Used*
> - observing
> - comparing
> - predicting

Guided Discovery

Background information for the teacher:
The density of a liquid is measured by the heaviness of a given volume. The molecules of a dense liquid are more tightly packed together.

Materials needed for each group:
baby food jar of one liquid (oil, soda pop, corn syrup, or milk)
grape
carrot slice
plastic toy
cork

Directions for the activity:
As a demonstration, test the four items in the water to see if they sink or float. Have students predict whether each item will float or sink in each liquid. Divide the class into four groups. Give each group one liquid substance and the four floating/sinking items that were tested in the water previously. Group members work together to test the four items and record their findings on the activity sheet.

Responding to Discovery

Each group should report the results of the discovery to the class. As the groups report their results, all students should record "float" and "sink" on the matrix.

Applications and Extensions

Students work at centers to explore the items in each of the different substances. Have students decide on additional items to test in the liquids. Students can also think of additional liquids to test.

> *Real-World Applications*
> - Name some liquids that are thick (gravy, soap, syrup, etc.).

0-7682-3370-4 *Inquiry Science*

Name _____

Floating and Sinking Substances

Our liquid was _____.

🐣 Draw what each item did when it was placed in the water.

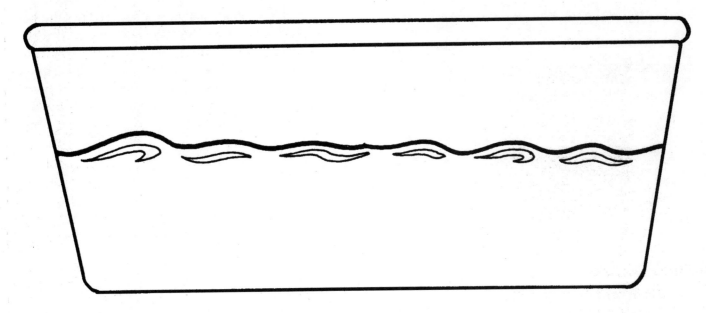

🐣 Listen to the results from the other groups.
🐣 Write float or sink in each square to complete the grid.

	Carrot	Cork	Toy	Grape
Corn syrup				
Soda pop				
Oil				
Milk				

 0-7682-3370-4 *Inquiry Science*

Float Your Clay Boat

Gearing Up

Put a ball of clay in the water. Ask students to describe what happened. One way to make the clay float, is to add full-length straws to the ball of clay like spokes on a bicycle. Place the clay and straws in the water and ask students to describe what happened. Challenge the students to think of another way to make the clay float. If students do not mention making a boat, bring the idea to their attention.

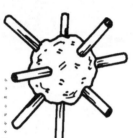

Process Skills Used
- observation
- measurement

Guided Discovery

Background information for the teacher:
Some materials are naturally buoyant. Some materials float only when they are made into buoyant shapes.

Materials needed for each group:
tub of water
2 oz. of clay
paper towels
balance scale
pennies
4 teddy bear counters

Directions for the activity:
Have each student use the balance scale to measure a piece of clay that is equal to the mass of 4 teddy bear counters. Students use their clay to design a boat shape and test the shape to find out whether it floats.

Allow the students to experiment with the clay and determine the best boat design. Using their best design, students test the number of pennies that the boat will hold before it sinks. Each student draws the boat design on the activity sheet and records the number of pennies it held. Then, challenge them to create another boat design. They test the number of pennies boat 2 will hold before it sinks and record boat design #2 on the activity sheet.

Responding to Discovery

Pose one of the following questions about the activity. Allow student partners to discuss the question. Ask some students to share their ideas with the whole class.

- What design held the most pennies?
- What attributes are important when designing a boat?
- Does your boat look like a real boat you have seen?

Applications and Extensions

Students test other items instead of pennies in their boat designs (paper clips, teddy bears, cubes). Predict the number of items the boat will hold.

Real-World Applications
- Look at various boat designs.
- Name toys and familiar objects that float.

0-7682-3370-4 *Inquiry Science*

Name _____

Float Your Clay Boat

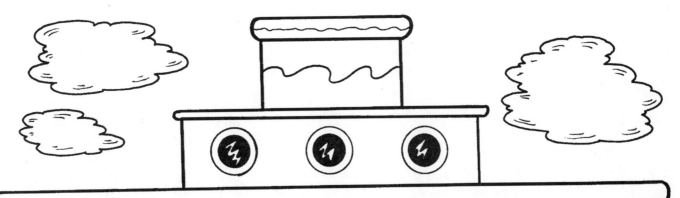

Boat Design #1

Boat Design #2

Number of pennies _____

Number of pennies _____

0-7682-3370-4 *Inquiry Science*

Floating Foil Boats

Gearing Up

Discuss the designs of the students' clay boats. Have students predict the greatest number of pennies that a foil boat might hold.

> ### Process Skills Used
> - predicting
> - experimenting

Guided Discovery

Background information for the teacher:
Some materials are naturally buoyant. Some materials float only when they are made into buoyant shapes.

Materials needed for each pair:
dishtub of water
2 square pieces of aluminum foil
paper towels
pennies
Post-It note

Directions for the activity:
Partners design a boat shape using the aluminum foil and test the shape to find out whether it floats. Then, they experiment with the foil boat to determine what shape floats the best. Students choose their best design. Partners test the number of pennies that the boat will hold before it sinks. Have students draw the boat design on the activity sheet. Then, students create another boat design. They test the number of pennies boat #2 will hold before it sinks. Draw boat design #2 on the activity sheet.

Responding to Discovery

Ask each student to write on a Post-It note the number of pennies that one of their boat designs held. Make a graph of the actual number of pennies that the boats held.

Discuss: Did your foil boat hold more or less than the clay boat? Was it easier to design the foil or the clay boat?

Applications and Extensions

Students propose and test other materials that could be used to make boats.

> ### Real-World Applications
> - What materials are used in ship building? Why do they use those materials?

0-7682-3370-4 *Inquiry Science*

Floating Foil Boats

Design a boat out of aluminum foil.

Draw your plan.

How many pennies do you think your boat will hold? _____

Build your boat. Add one penny at a time to the boat until the boat dips under water.

Draw your boat in the water holding pennies.

Design a second foil boat. Draw it here.

How many pennies did it hold before it sank? _____

How many pennies did it hold before it sank? _____

Load the Boat

Gearing Up

As a demonstration, float a Styrofoam bowl in a clear tank of water. Then ask the students to guess how many teddy bears you can put into this bowl before it sinks. Place one teddy bear counter in the bowl to show what you mean. Students write their predictions on Post-It notes and stick them on the chalkboard. Volunteers may organize the notes from the smallest to the largest number. Ask students questions about the numbers. "Which number is the greatest? Smallest? Can you find an even number? Show me a number that is greater than 20." Next, students add one teddy bear at a time to the bowl until the bowl sinks. Compare the students' predictions to the actual number of teddy bears.

Process Skills Used
- measurement
- predicting

Guided Discovery

Background information for the teacher:
Capacity is the amount of cargo a floating vessel can bear without sinking. Three variables affect the capacity of a boat—its size, its shape, and the material that it is made from.

Materials needed for each group:
teddy bear counters
dishtub of water
various vessels:
    plastic cup
    meat tray
    egg carton
    margarine tub

Directions for the activity:
On the activity sheet, each student predicts the number of teddy bears each vessel will hold. Students put the teddy bear counters in each vessel until it sinks. Count the number of counters. Record the results on the activity sheet.

Responding to Discovery

Students make pirate hats out of tan construction paper. They should write on the back of their hats one sentence about the activity. Gather students in a circle with their pirate hats on. Make up a story about pirates. The teacher will begin the story with the sentence, "Long, long ago, a pirate ship sailed with a special cargo . . ." Each student adds a sentence.

Applications and Extensions

Have students bring in additional containers to use in the experiment. They can also use other items as cargo.

Real-World Applications
- Cargo ships sit lower in the water when they have a heavier load.

Load the Boat

Draw each vessel.

Vessel #1

I predict _____ teddy bears.

It held _____ teddy bears.

Vessel #2

I predict _____ teddy bears.

It held _____ teddy bears.

Vessel #3

I predict _____ teddy bears.

It held _____ teddy bears.

Vessel #4

I predict _____ teddy bears.

It held _____ teddy bears.

What Makes a Good Float?

Gearing Up

Sing "Little Boat"
(to the tune of "Twinkle, Twinkle").

> Gently floating, little boat,
> Gently floating on the sea.
> Out upon the ocean wide,
> Flowing with the evening tide,
> Gently floating, little boat,
> Gently floating on the sea.

Before this day, invite students to bring in toy boats, pictures of boats, and boat models. In a learning center, allow students to sort and classify the boats according to different properties. Make a class graph. Discuss the graph.

Process Skills Used
- sorting
- classifying
- exploring
- graphing

Guided Discovery

Background information for the teacher:
Some materials are naturally buoyant; other materials float only when they are made into buoyant shapes. The mass of a boat and the material from which it is made are both factors that affect its buoyancy and its capacity.

Materials needed for each group:
variety of toy boats
dishtub of water
straws

Directions for the activity:
Students predict which toy boats are most seaworthy. Write their observations about shapes, sizes, and materials. Challenge students to move the boats through the water without touching them. Encourage students to be creative in their ways to move the boats. Students write about their findings on the boat shape on page 25.

Responding to Discovery

Students pick their three favorite boats. Survey the class to find the most popular boat on the activity sheets. Students can name the boats and keep a tally while classmates share their favorites. Discuss the results.

Applications and Extensions

Students hold a boat race in which they may not touch their boats.

Real-World Applications
- What types of boats and ships travel in the oceans?

Name _____

What Makes a Good Float?

I observed . . .

My Favorite Boats

Draw your three favorite toy boats.

0-7682-3370-4 *Inquiry Science*

Floating Liquids

Gearing Up

Pour six different liquids into six baby food jars. Give students the opportunity to observe the way the liquids move, smell, and feel. Sort the liquids according to color, movement, and other characteristics.

> *Process Skills Used*
> * observation
> * exploring

Guided Discovery

Background information for the teacher:
The density of an object is a measurement of its heaviness per volume. Density is a relationship between an object's mass and its volume.

Materials needed for each group:
corn syrup
dishwashing liquid
vegetable oil
rubbing alcohol
glycerin
water
baby food jars

Directions for the activity:
Pick two liquids. Predict what will happen when the two liquids are combined. (Students will discover that one liquid will sink to the bottom or the liquids will mix.) Gently pour the two liquids together into a baby-food jar. Draw the combined liquids on the activity sheet. Repeat this procedure with another two liquids.

Gather the class together. Combine all six ingredients in a tall, narrow cylinder. Combine them in the following order: corn syrup, dishwashing liquid, vegetable oil, rubbing alcohol, glycerin, and water.

Add small items to the cylinder (cork, marble, paper clip, etc.). Observe where the objects rest in the layers. On the activity sheet, students should draw and describe what they observed.

Responding to Discovery

Have one student describe one of the liquids while the other students guess which one it is.

Play "Walk, Freeze, Talk" to provide students with an opportunity to share what they have learned about liquids. Students should "walk" around the room, "freeze" when the teacher says the word and find a partner, then "talk" about the question the teacher poses.

* Which liquids floated on others?
* Why did some liquids go to the bottom of the jar?
* Why did the objects float at different levels in the cylinder?

Applications and Extensions

Have students think of other liquids to test for their ability to "float."

> *Real-World Applications*
> * Read about the damage caused by oil spills on the oceans. What happens to the animals that live in the area? How do people clean up a spill?

Name _____

Floating Liquids

We put two liquids together:

I put in _____ and _____ .

I put in _____ and _____ .

We combined all the liquids together. (Draw and label the results.)

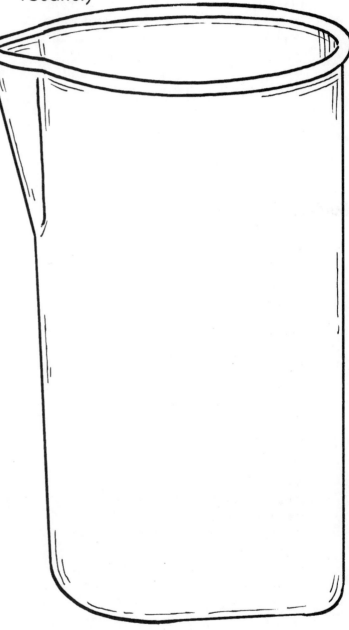

This is what I found out:

_____

_____

0-7682-3370-4 *Inquiry Science*

Which Water?

Gearing Up

Have students use their five senses to ob-serve the differences and similarities be-tween salt water and fresh water. Give each student small cups of water and salt water. On chart paper, write the following headings: *Sight, Touch, Smell, Hearing,* and *Taste.* Discuss how the waters are similar and different in each category. Record the stu-dents' observations.

> ### *Process Skills Used*
> - observation
> - predicting
> - experimenting

Guided Discovery

Background information for the teacher:
Salt water is denser than fresh water. The denser a liquid, the easier objects float in it. The ocean contains salt, which is why it is easier to float in the ocean than in fresh water.

Materials needed for each group:
2 deep bowls or mugs of water
kosher salt
an egg
a carrot slice
a shell
a paper clip

Directions for the activity:
Students add ¼ cup salt to one bowl of water and dissolve. Leave the other bowl of water plain. Students predict whether each given item will sink or float in fresh and salt water. Students should test each item in the fresh water first and then the salt water. Record the results on the activity sheet.

Responding to Discovery

Discuss the results of the discovery. Have students paint a message with salt water with a paintbrush on black construction paper. The papers should be left in the sun to dry. Then, students can read and share their messages.

Applications and Extensions

Place ½ cup of water and ½ cup of salt water in the sun. Observe what happens over a period of one week. What is left in the bottom of the glasses?

Have students bring in other items from home to test in the salt water. Record which items sink and which float.

> ### *Real-World Applications*
> - What animals live in the ocean?
> - When you swim in the ocean, it is easier to float.

Name _____

Which Water?

Fresh Water

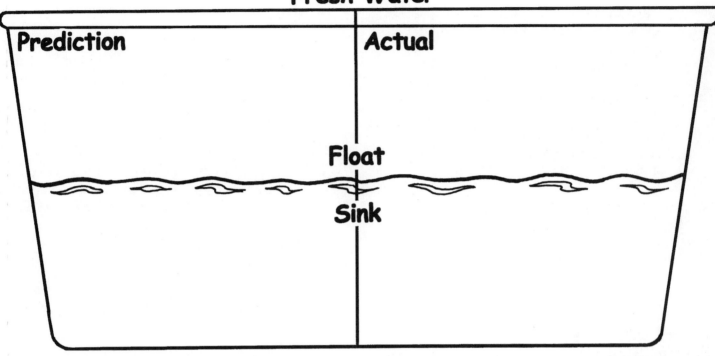

Prediction | Actual

Float

Sink

Salt Water

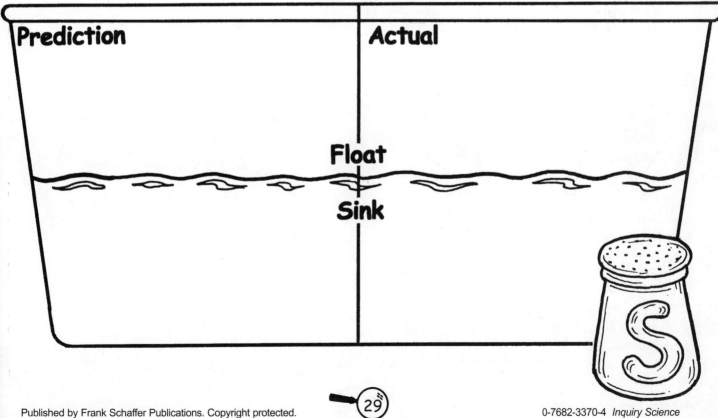

Prediction | Actual

Float

Sink

0-7682-3370-4 *Inquiry Science*

Ice Cube Float

Gearing Up

Place an ice cube inside a plastic bag inside a thin paper bag (such as a lunch bag). Pass the bag around for the students to feel without seeing. Ask them to guess what it is.

As a demonstration, show students how to make two ice cubes stick together. Sprinkle salt on one cube, put a second cube on top of the salt, and pick up the cube. Ask the students to propose explanations.

> *Process Skills Used*
> - observing
> - exploring
> - communicating

Guided Discovery

Background information for the teacher:
Water expands when it freezes. Ice is lighter than water because the water particles expand in the freezing process. Salt lowers the temperature at which water freezes. The salted ice melts and refreezes to the second cube.

Materials needed:
ice cubes
salt
small plastic bottle
aluminum foil
dishtubs
water
magnifying lenses

Directions for the first activity:
Fill the bottle to the top with warm water and wrap aluminum foil around the opening. Place the bottle in the freezer and move on to the second activity while it freezes.

When the water is frozen, students make observations about the bottle. They should notice that the ice is coming out of the top of the bottle because the water expanded when it froze.

Directions for the second activity:

Give each student an ice cube and a magnifying lens. They should draw the ice cube on the activity sheet. Next, have students place their ice cubes in water. Observe how much of the ice cube floats above the surface. Students draw it on the activity sheet.

Instruct the students to try to push the ice cubes under the water and observe. Fill a clear glass to the rim with water and ice. Have students predict what will happen when the ice cubes melt. Will the water spill over? Students should observe and discuss what happens.

Responding to Discovery

Brainstorm words related to ice. Students then create "ice" poems. They could use the following format:

> Ice
> Hard, cold,
> Slippery, melting, dripping,
> Ice.

Applications and Extensions

Hold an ice cube melting race: Each student group will be given an ice cube with various materials (salt, straw, paper towels, and other materials proposed by the class). Groups will be challenged to melt the ice cube in the shortest amount of time.

> *Real-World Applications*
> - How do you prevent ice cubes from watering down drinks?

0-7682-3370-4 *Inquiry Science*

Ice Cube Float

Draw the ice cube under the magnifying lens.

Draw the ice cube in the water.

Draw the bottle of ice.

Why doesn't the ice cube sink?

_____

_____

_____

Explain what you think happened.

_____

_____

_____

What happened when the ice melted in the full glass of water? Explain.

_____

_____

_____

Weighing Fruit

Gearing Up

Brainstorm types of fruit. Write the fruits on a class graph. Ask students to draw their favorites and glue their fruits to the graph. Discuss the graph data.

Process Skills Used
- graphing
- predicting
- measuring

Guided Discovery

Background information for the teacher:
When an object is placed in the water, some water is displaced or moved. It might go up higher in the container or spill over the edge. The amount of water that moves is equal to the amount the object weighs. This concept is called *Archimedes' Principle*. Read *Mr. Archimedes' Bath* by Pamela Allen.

Materials needed for each group:
water
peach
lemon
plum
apple
2-cup measuring cup
ounce scale

Directions for the activity:

Work in teams. Fill the measuring cup up to the 8 oz. or 1-cup mark. Have students predict whether each fruit will sink or float. Add one of the fruits to the water and record the level of the water on the activity sheet. Students use a kitchen scale to measure the mass of the fruit. Does the number of ounces of displaced liquid equal the number of ounces on the scale?

Responding to Discovery

Students can create rhymes or riddles about fruit. They can draw or paint an accompanying picture. Fold one third of the paper over so other students can open the fold and find the answer to the riddle inside.

Example: *I am red, juicy, and crunchy. What am I?*

Applications and Extensions

- Make fruit salad.
- Students can test other items to see how much they weigh.

Real-World Applications
- Watch the water level rise when you get in the bathtub.

Name _____

Weighing Fruit

Prediction: **sink/float**

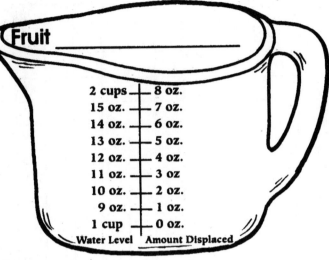

The water went up to _____ .

The fruit weighs _____ .

Prediction: **sink/float**

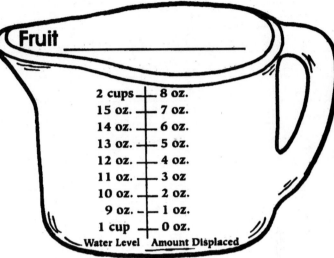

The water went up to _____ .

The fruit weighs _____ .

Prediction: **sink/float**

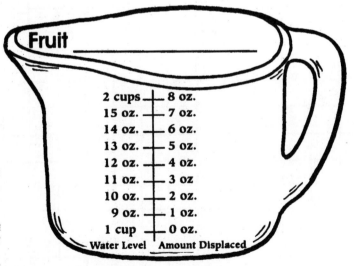

The water went up to _____ .

The fruit weighs _____ .

Prediction: **sink/float**

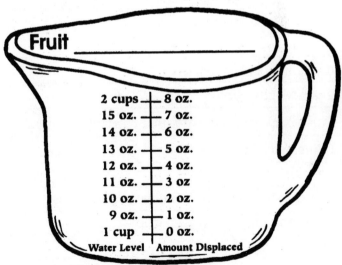

The water went up to _____ .

The fruit weighs _____ .

0-7682-3370-4 *Inquiry Science*

Performance-Based Assessment

3 = Exceeds expectations
2 = Consistently meets expectations
1 = Below expectations

Student Names

Lesson Investigation Discovery

Lesson 1: Water Wonders											
Lesson 2: Sink or Float											
Lesson 3: Sinking Floaters											
Lesson 4: Floating Sinkers											
Lesson 5: Shapes That Float											
Lesson 6: Floating and Sinking Substances											
Lesson 7: Float Your Clay Boat											
Lesson 8: Floating Foil Boats											
Lesson 9: Load the Boat											
Lesson 10: What Makes a Good Float?											
Lesson 11: Floating Liquids											
Lesson 12: Which Water?											
Lesson 13: Ice Cube Float											
Lesson 14: Weighing Fruit											

Specific Lesson Skills

Can make reasonable predictions.											
Can make detailed observations.											
Can propose an explanation.											
Can follow directions.											
Displays curiosity.											
Can work cooperatively with a partner or group.											
Participates in discussions.											
Can complete a grid.											
Can classify objects in meaningful categories.											
Can communicate through writing and drawing.											
Can apply what is learned to real-world situations.											

0-7682-3370-4 *Inquiry Science*

Soil

Geologist on the Go

Gearing Up

Ask students to name the biggest thing they have ever touched. After they have shared their responses, tell them that they have all touched something much, much larger—the earth.

Guided Discovery

Background for the teacher:

Geology is the study of the history and structure of the earth. The earth is made up of three major layers—the core, mantle, and crust. The crust is only the thin outer covering of the earth, about 4–22 miles (6–35 km) deep. Geologists learn about the center of the earth by studying seismic waves from earthquakes.

Materials needed for the class:

model of the inside of earth (picture or physical model)

a large ball, such as a basketball

30 feet of green or brown ribbon or streamer

10 feet of red ribbon

Directions for the discovery:

Describe the layers of the earth as you display the model. Then, given the following descriptions, have the students act out the layers.

Core: Have one student stand in the center of the room and hold a large ball. The inner core of the earth is a solid nickel and iron ball that is under great pressure from the mass of the earth.

Have 3–4 students circle the center student to represent the outer core which is the only liquid layer of the earth. The outer core is made of liquid nickel and other substances. The circling students can hold the red streamer to represent the very hot temperature of the core.

Mantle: Have 10–12 students surround the core facing out, possibly in two layers or grouped tightly. Some students can be squatting to represent the stony materials that make up this thickest layer of the earth.

Crust: A circle of the remaining students move around the mantle chanting softly, "moving plates." They are holding a green or brown streamer to represent the growing materials or the soil found in the crust.

Although the crust is relatively thin, it is the only layer from which geologists have actually been able to obtain samples. Allow the students to study a crust sample and describe what they see in it. (Dig about a foot down and collect a sample of earth that may contain rocks, plant or animal life, and decomposed material.)

Responding to Discovery

Sing this song to the tune of "Baby Bumble Bee":
I'm digging up a big hole in the earth.
Won't geologists be so proud of me!
I'm digging up a big hole in the crust.
Wow! Look what I see . . .

Discuss what the geologist might see in or on the crust. Students may create pictures to share their ideas of what might be in the top layer of the earth.

Name _____

Geologist on the Go

The earth has 3 layers—the core, the mantle, and the crust. Draw the layers:

The Earth

Here are some things I saw in the crust sample of the earth . . .

0-7682-3370-4 *Inquiry Science*

Rock On!

Gearing Up

Prior to this lesson, have students collect rocks from their neighborhoods. Also, have a collection of rocks available to supplement theirs. Divide the students into groups of four. Each group should have a collection of rocks spread out on the table in front of them. Each student in the group should secretly select and draw a rock from the collection without picking it up. One by one, students share their pictures and verbal descriptions with the group. The other group members try to identify the rock in the collection.

Process Skills Used
- observing
- communicating
- classifying

Guided Discovery

Background for the teacher:

Rock is found in the crust of the earth. Rock may be covered with soil and vegetation or visible on mountains and hills. Rock may wear down and become smaller and rougher or smoother from erosion and other forces.

Materials available to each student:

a variety of rocks   balance scale
magnifying lens

unifix cubes or gram masses for weighing

Directions for the discovery:

Have each student select one rock to study. Have students look carefully with magnifying lenses to make observations and draw their rocks when wet and dry.

Next, have students gather 3–5 rocks each. They should use the balance scale to order their rocks from heaviest to lightest.

Students should then sort their rocks and record how they sorted them on the student handout.

Responding to Discovery

Have students work in groups with the rock collections to make a "rock train." A rock train is a line of rocks—each rock has one attribute in common with the rock before it. Put one rock in the middle of the table. All the students should think of descriptive words for that rock. Next, have a student place a rock next to the original rock and give two or three descriptive words. This rock should have one characteristic in common with the first rock. Students take turns adding rocks with one attribute in common with the preceding rock.

Applications and Extensions

Students can decorate rocks with paint; adding eyes, hair, and other facial features to make pet rocks or rock groups. Decorated rocks may make nice gifts for friends or parents.

Real-World Applications
- Using rocks as tools
- Rock collecting

0-7682-3370-4 *Inquiry Science*

Name _____

Rock On!

Draw your rock and write some observations.

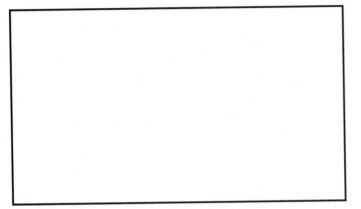

_____

_____

_____

_____

_____

Draw your rocks from heaviest to lightest.

Draw how you sorted your rocks.

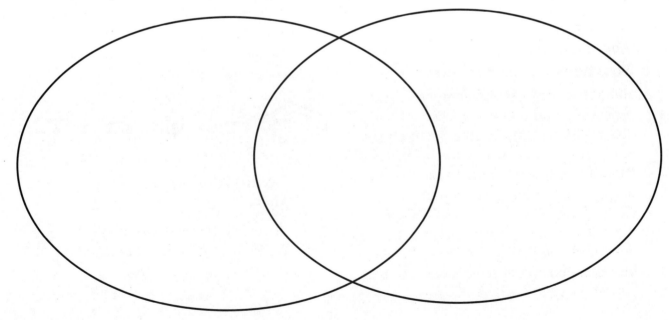

0-7682-3370-4 *Inquiry Science*

Shake Rocks to Soil

Gearing Up

Give each group of students five interesting rocks that vary in size. Ask each group to order their rocks by size. Discuss why rocks come in different sizes.

> ### Process Skills Used
> - observing
> - classifying
> - making a model

Guided Discovery

Background for the teacher:

Rocks wear down into soil through erosion. Erosion, or weathering, can be caused by wind or water. The force of wind or water can wear away rock into smaller pieces. Wind and water can also cause small rocks to rub together and wear down or break apart.

Materials needed for each student:

sandstone and limestone chunks

plastic jar with lid

water

Directions for the discovery:

Have students feel and compare the sandstone and limestone. Discuss observations. Have each student choose one stone and draw a picture of it. They should fill their jars with about 1 cup of water and add the limestone or sandstone. After students cover and shake their jars 50 times, they should draw what is in the jar. Discuss how the water has changed. Then, have students open their jars, pour the water through a fine strainer, and feel the stone inside. They can record their observations on the activity sheet.

Responding to Discovery

Discuss (and try out) what would happen if you put sand in the jar before shaking the stone in water.

Sing the following song to the tune of "Hokie Pokie":

You put the rocks right in, you put the rocks right in,

You put the water in, and you shake it all around.

We're showing how weathering and erosion come about.

That's what it's all about.

Applications and Extensions

Try the experiment with other types of rocks.

Use white glue to make a design on black construction paper. Rub two sandstone rocks over the paper to create sand pictures.

> ### Real-World Applications
> - Why are rocks different sizes?
> - How was the Grand Canyon formed?
> - Show how a rock tumbler works.

0-7682-3370-4 *Inquiry Science*

Name _____

Shake Rocks to Soil

My rock:

Before   **After**

My rock felt _____   My rock felt _____

Draw what you saw in the jar.

Write what you observed.

_____

_____

_____

_____

_____

_____

_____

_____

_____

_____

0-7682-3370-4 *Inquiry Science*

Ice Rocks

Gearing Up

Before students arrive, put an ice cube in a sealed plastic bag. Put the plastic bag inside a dark bag. Tell the students that you would like them to discover what is inside the mystery bag by asking you questions. Tell them you are only able to answer "yes" or "no." After they have guessed, tell them that today they are going to learn about a special kind of ice called a glacier.

Process Skills Used
- observing
- communicating
- making a model

Guided Discovery

Background for the teacher:

Water expands when it freezes. Ice can be a very powerful source of erosion, or weathering. As ice-age glaciers receded, they formed major landforms, such as the Great Lakes. We can see the effects of freezing and thawing on roads in cold climates. After a winter of freezing and thawing, there are many potholes on the roads.

Materials needed for each group:

water	Styrofoam cup	dirt
sand	limestone	clay

Directions for the discovery:

Give each group a small cup. Students should write their group name on the cup and fill the cup half full with water and a teaspoon each of sand and soil. Put the cups in the freezer and ask the students to predict what their cups will look like tomorrow.

The next day, have students observe their frozen water and remove it from the cup. Discuss how the water expanded as it froze. Then, each group should flatten a piece of clay on a flat surface. They should rub the sandy ice across the smooth clay and observe. Discuss and have students record their hypotheses about what happened and how a glacier might act similarly on land. Then, have students rub the ice over the piece of limestone and make observations of the effect of the sandy ice on the stone.

Responding to Discovery

Sing the following song to the tune of "Farmer in the Dell":

The ice moves on land.
The ice moves on land.
Did you know the glacier will go?
The ice moves on land.
The ice smooths the rocks.
The ice smooths the rocks.
On the go with the glacial flow,
The ice smooths the rocks.

Challenge the students to create another verse to explain why rocks weather from ice.

Applications and Extensions

Have students design an experiment to test various types of rocks to see if they can create a situation where weathering from ice occurs.

Real-World Applications
- glacial movement
- ice on the roads

0-7682-3370-4 *Inquiry Science*

Ice Rocks

Draw the clay.

Before the ice

After the ice

Draw the limestone.

Before the ice

After the ice

0-7682-3370-4 *Inquiry Science*

Diggin' Dirt

Gearing Up

After students come in from outside, tell them that someone has brought something into the classroom and you want an explanation. Tell them the evidence can be found on the floor mat by the door (dirt). Ask the students to propose explanations for how the dirt could have gotten there.

> ### Process Skills Used
> • observing

Guided Discovery

Background for the teacher:

Soil forms as rocks and organic materials break down over a period of time. Weathering and other forces break rock down into sand. Organic material found in soil is made from decaying plants and animals.

Materials needed for each group:

two containers for soil samples

water

Styrofoam or aluminum tray

Directions for the discovery:

Have students go on a dirt hunt around the school grounds. Each group may collect two samples of dirt. On each container, they should write the location they found the sample. Back in the classroom, each student should draw a detailed picture of one soil sample on his/her activity sheet. Ask the following questions to encourage students to write detailed observations about the dirt:

• What does the soil look like?
• What color is it?
• How does it smell?
• How does it feel?
• What is the texture?

Responding to Discovery

Have students make mud pies with their soil samples. Each student puts half a cup of soil in a Styrofoam tray and adds water until the soil becomes mud. They can sculpt the mud into interesting shapes. Discuss which soil samples seem to make the best mud. Brainstorm words that describe mud. Students can use the words to complete a poem about mud.

I like mud.

Mud is _____ , _____ ,
_____ .

I like mud.

Display mud pies and poems together.

Applications and Extensions

Have students predict where mud puddles will form on the school grounds. After a rain, they can look for puddles and measure them over a period of days until the puddles are gone.

> ### Real-World Applications
> • What are the benefits of mud?
> • Visit a site where digging has exposed different layers of soil.

0-7682-3370-4 Inquiry Science

Name _____

Diggin' Dirt

This is what my dirt looks like.

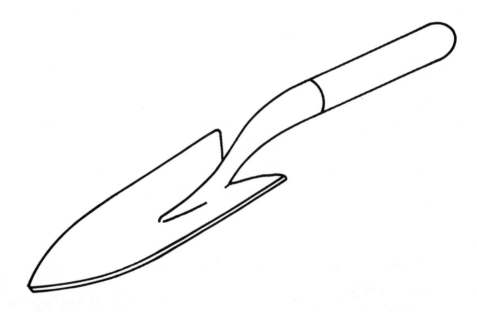

I observed _____

_____

_____

_____ .

0-7682-3370-4 *Inquiry Science*

What's in Soil?

Gearing Up

Give each group of students a sample of rich garden soil. Challenge them to use the equipment provided (see materials listed below) to separate the soil into the following categories: large pieces, medium pieces, small pieces, and things that were once alive. Ask students to describe how they tried to separate the soil. Discuss how difficult this was.

> *Process Skills Used*
> - observing
> - classifying
> - problem solving

Guided Discovery

Background for the teacher:

Soil contains many particles including sand, small stones, silt, clay, dead plants, and dead animals.

Materials needed for each student:

paper cup of soil

toothpicks

tweezers (shared)

paper plate

plastic jar with lid (one per group)

water

Directions for the discovery:

Tell students that you have a simpler method for separating the soil. Have each group half fill the plastic jar with soil and nearly fill the jar with water. Someone should close the jar securely. Group members can take turns shaking the soil and water about 20 times each.

Observe the contents of the jar as they settle for several minutes. As the soil and water are settling, students can discuss predictions of what the jar will look like when it has finished settling. After about 30 minutes, each student should draw and label the actual soil layers on the activity sheet.

Responding to Discovery

Use the "line-talk strategy" to have students discuss the given questions about soil. Students stand in two lines facing each other. Every pair of students discusses the question given by the teacher. Then the first person in one line moves to the back of the line. Now new pairs are matched to discuss the next question. Questions:

- Are all the particles of soil the same size?

- What layer was the thickest?

- What layer contains the largest pieces in the soil?

- Did you see anything in the soil that might have been alive?

Applications and Extensions

Have students write to friends or relatives that live in other parts of the country to request soil samples. When the samples arrive, students should mark the locations of the soil on the map and observe and compare the samples.

> *Real-World Applications*
> - Learn what geologists do.

What's in Soil?

This is what I found in the soil sample.

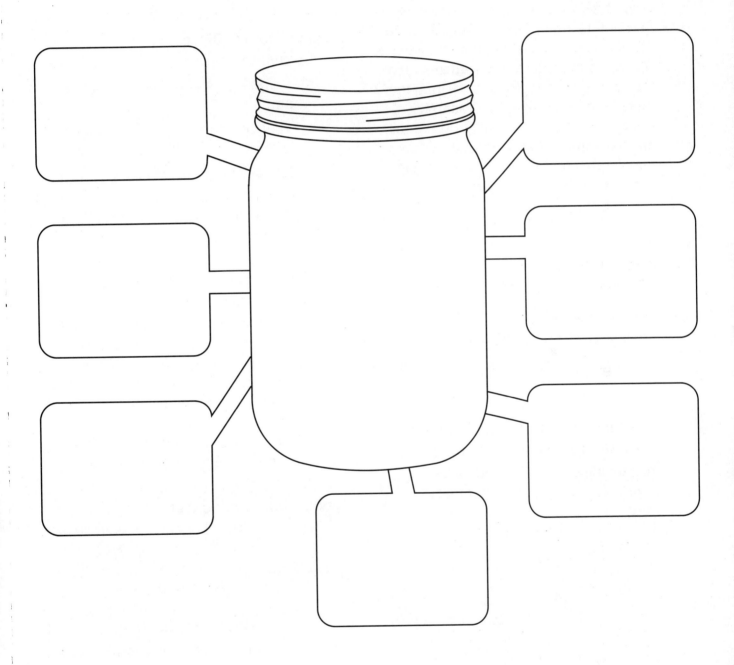

0-7682-3370-4 *Inquiry Science*

The Scoop on Soil

Gearing Up

Before class, collect three different soil samples from the school grounds (sandy playground, rich garden, and grassy area). Tell the students that you have three mystery soils. Their job is to find out as much as they can about the soil to make a decision about where the soil came from. Take the students on a tour of the school grounds, visiting the three areas from where the samples were taken. Have students observe the areas carefully, taking notes and drawing pictures of the clues that will help them identify the soil locations.

> ### Process Skills Used
> - observing
> - predicting
> - communicating

Guided Discovery

Background for the teacher:

Soil contains many particles including sand, small stones, silt, clay, dead plants, and dead animals.

Materials needed for each group:

mystery soils, labeled A, B, and C
magnifying glass   toothpicks
tweezers   paper plate
water
three plastic jars with lids

Directions for the discovery:

Allow the groups time to observe the samples carefully, looking for clues and taking notes that will help them identify from which location the samples were taken. When the students have made their observations, they can place the samples in jars and add water. They should cover the jar and shake it thoroughly. After the soil settles (about 15 minutes), students can compare the layers of the three samples.

Responding to Discovery

Discuss the following questions:

- Do the layers of the soils look the same?

- What component is the same in all three samples? What is different?

- How do the particles feel in the three samples?

- Do you see anything in the soil that might have been alive?

- Do all the soil samples have the same number of layers?

Group students randomly to discuss how they matched the soil samples to the appropriate areas. The students in each group will discuss what clues helped them make their decision. After the groups meet, the teacher can reveal the exact location of each sample. Hold a class discussion about what clues in the area matched the clues in the samples.

Applications and Extensions

Test the pH level of each of your soils.

> ### Real-World Applications
> - Learn about the different classifications of soil types (found in an encyclopedia).

0-7682-3370-4 *Inquiry Science*

The Scoop on Soil

Here is what I observed in each area.

1 _____	2 _____	3 _____

Here is what I observed in each soil sample:

A	B	C

Draw lines to match the areas with the soil samples.

 0-7682-3370-4 *Inquiry Science*

Making Soil

Gearing Up

Share this poem with the class.

I like soil!

I dig in the dirt most every day,

When I go out to run and play.

It's best as mud—all wet and black.

I look for worms, then put them back.

Sometimes my mom will say,

"Please don't get dirty today!"

But, I like soil.

> ### *Process Skills Used*
> - observing
> - predicting
> - comparing

Guided Discovery

Background for the teacher:

Soil contains many particles including sand, small stones, silt, clay, dead plants, and dead animals.

Materials needed for each group:

soil sample	sand	leaves
grass	stems	twigs
paper plate	water	rock
two plastic jars with lids		

Directions for the discovery:

Students use the following recipe to "make" soil.

Recipe for homemade soil:

- Put 1/2 cup of sand on a paper plate.
- Break up into small pieces: dried leaves, grass, stems, and twigs. (Amounts will vary. Allow students to use their judgement.)
- Grind the pieces with a rock.
- Add the pieces to the sand, stir in a little water to dampen, and mix well.

Have students compare the homemade soil sample to the natural soil sample. Then have them put the soil samples in jars, add water, cover, and shake. Let the contents settle and have students observe the similarities and differences between the two soils.

Responding to Discovery

Use the "my-buddy strategy" for discussing the discovery. First, the teacher asks a question. Then, students will walk around the room and think about the question. When the teacher says "stop," each student turns to the closest classmate and says, "my buddy." The buddies then discuss the question. Possible questions:

- How is your soil the same as the natural soil?
- How is your soil different from the natural soil?
- Did the soils have the same number of layers?
- Were the layers the same thickness?
- Why do you think there were differences?
- Could you ever make a soil that was exactly like a natural soil?

Applications and Extensions

Have students make up a homemade soil recipe based on their observations.

> ### *Real-World Applications*
> - What lives in the soil?

0-7682-3370-4 *Inquiry Science*

Name _____

Making Soil

Soil Sample

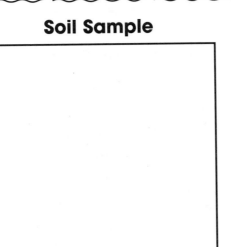

My Soil

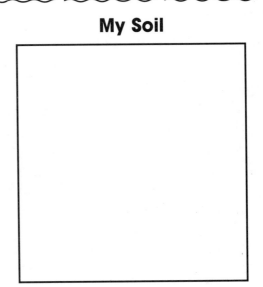

Shake the jars of soil. Wait. Draw what you see.

Natural soil and water

My Soil and water

0-7682-3370-4 *Inquiry Science*

Soil Soaking Test

Gearing Up

Bring students outside to feel a clump of soil. Ask them whether they think it contains water. Can they see or smell the water? Ask them how they can prove that there is water in the soil. Have students put the clump in a paper cup. Back in the classroom, students should cover their cups with plastic wrap and secure with a rubber band. Have students leave their cups in a sunny spot for a day. Allow students to check their cups throughout the day to see if there is any evidence of water in the soil.

> ### Process Skills Used
> - observing
> - predicting
> - making a model

Guided Discovery

Background for the teacher:

Different soils hold different amounts of water. Some types of soil absorb water quickly, then hold the water inside like a sponge. This might give plants a better chance of using some of the water. Other types of soil allow water to drain completely through in just a few seconds.

Materials needed for each group:

three soil samples, from rich soil to sand

three coffee filters

three measuring cups

timer

three 2-liter soda-pop bottles

Before class, cut the top one-third off each bottle and turn it upside down to be used as a funnel.

Directions for the discovery:

Students place a coffee filter in each funnel portion of the bottle. Then, they should put 1/4 cup (59 mL) of soil in each filter. Students measure 1/2 cup (118 mL) of water into each measuring cup and pour the water over all three soil samples at the same time and start the timer. Have students time how long it takes the water to drain from each sample. Students should record their observations and discuss why the water acted differently in the different samples. Ask students to look at the soils carefully. Are they blocky or chunky? What color are they? What plant matter is visible? Do the soils feel light or heavy?

Responding to Discovery

Discuss the following questions with the class:

- Which soil would you want if you were a gardener?
- What might happen if the soil was full of water and it started to rain?
- Why do puddles form?
- What might make the soils different colors?

Applications and Extensions

Have students design an experiment to clean the water that drained through the soil samples.

> ### Real-World Applications
> - What are different ways farmers keep their crops moist?

0-7682-3370-4 *Inquiry Science*

Name _____

Soil Soaking Test

Draw what happened when you poured water over each sample.

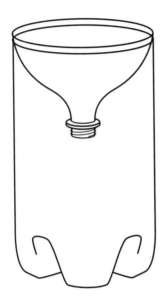

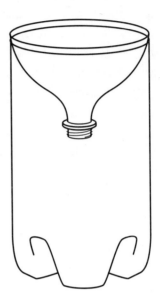

Soil Sample 1 Time: _____

Observations: _____

_____

Soil Sample 2 Time: _____

Observations: _____

_____

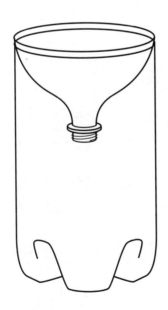

Soil Sample 3
Time: _____

Observations: _____

_____

_____

_____

0-7682-3370-4 *Inquiry Science*

The Heavy on Soil

Gearing Up

Pick two items from the classroom. Tell students that you can predict which item is heavier by holding one item in each hand. Demonstrate. Next, put the two items on the balance scale to prove to the students that you were correct. Have students try with a variety of objects to compare mass with their hands and then the balance scale.

Process Skills Used

- observing
- predicting
- measuring
- graphing

Guided Discovery

Background for the teacher:

The ingredients in soil can vary depending on the location of the soil. The composition of the soil affects the mass of the soil. For example, humus (decayed vegetable and animal matter used to enrich nutrients in soil) is much lighter than clay.

Materials needed for each group:

soil samples, from rich soil to sand

balance scale

several pennies

paper cups

measuring cups

graph paper

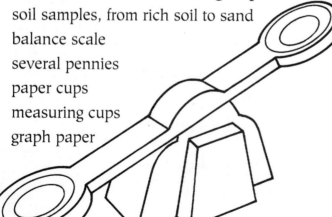

Directions for the discovery:

Each group of students should measure 1/2 cup (118 mL) of three different soil samples into paper cups. Label the samples (1, 2, and 3). Group members can first pick up each sample and predict which is the lightest or heaviest. Then, have students compare the samples on the balance scale. Finally, students can place a soil sample on one side of the balance scale and place pennies on the other until the scale balances. They should count the number of pennies and record the results on the record sheet.

Responding to Discovery

Discuss why some soils might weigh more than others. Have each group make a graph comparing the number of pennies needed to balance each soil sample. Then, have the groups compare graphs. They can discuss similarities and differences in their results.

Applications and Extensions

Compare the mass of pure humus with pure sand.

Real-World Applications

- Composting can add organic material to soil.

0-7682-3370-4 *Inquiry Science*

The Heavy on Soil

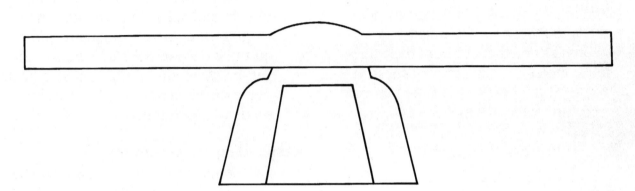

Soil #1 _____ pennies

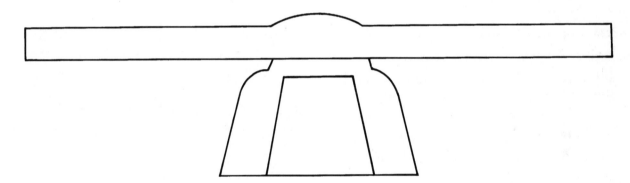

Soil #2 _____ pennies

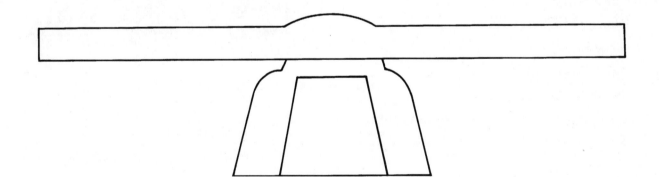

Soil #3 _____ pennies

55

0-7682-3370-4 *Inquiry Science*

Some Soil for Planting

Gearing Up

Display a marigold plant in a pot. Ask students to brainstorm what this plant needs to grow and stay healthy. Ask students to predict which of their three soil samples from the previous lesson would be the best for planting marigold seeds and why.

> *Process Skills Used*
> * observing
> * predicting
> * measuring
> * controlling variables

Guided Discovery

Background for the teacher:

Soil provides nutrients for plants to grow. Soil is the foundation of the food chain. Plants obtain their nutrients from soil and many animals get their nutrients from plants. Rich soil contains decomposed remnants of the plants (and animals) it fed.

Materials needed for each group:

soil samples, from rich soil to sand

paper cups

marigold seeds

water

Directions for the discovery:

Students fill three paper cups with soil samples from the three different areas of the school grounds described in "The Scoop on Soil" (pages 48–49). They should carefully label each cup. Follow the directions on the seed packet and have students plant the same number of marigold seeds in each cup. They should water the cups equally and put all three cups in the same area so they get the same amount of light and heat. Ask each student to predict which seeds will sprout first.

Responding to Discovery

On the record sheet, have students tally the predictions of their classmates. Make a class graph from the results. Students can observe and measure the seedlings in the different soils until they become adult plants.

Sometime between Day 12 and Day 16, have students draw and label each soil sample.

Applications and Extensions

Plant a garden on the school grounds.

> *Real-World Applications*
> * What are natural fertilizers?
> * Learn about food chains.

0-7682-3370-4 *Inquiry Science*

Some Soil for Planting

Prediction: I think Soil Sample # ____ will produce the first flower.

Write the measurement of each seedling and record comments.

Day 16			
Day 14			
Day 12			
Day 10			
Day 8			
Day 6			
Day 4			
Day 2			
	Soil Sample #1	**Soil Sample #2**	**Soil Sample #3**

Survey your friends to find out what soil they think will produce the first flower. Put tally marks in the boxes to count their predictions.

Soil Sample #1	**Soil Sample #2**	**Soil Sample #3**

Soil Erosion

Gearing Up

Return to the three areas on the school grounds studied on pages 48–49 (sandy playground, rich garden, grassy area). Use a garden hose or watering can to soak the ground in the three areas. Have the students observe what happens in each of the areas. Discuss with them why the water does or does not have an impact on the soil. Discuss the features of the soil and the surrounding materials.

> **Process Skills Used**
> - observing
> - measuring
> - modeling

Guided Discovery

Background for the teacher:

Erosion is caused by natural forces. Weathering can be caused by wind, water, or temperature. Erosion can be modified by the use of the earth. Plants can stabilize the soil, while traffic can break it down more quickly.

Materials needed for each group:

samples of potting soil and sand

aluminum tray	craft sticks
paper cup	rocks
twigs	leaves

Directions for the discovery:

Students will fill the bottom of the aluminum tray with about an inch of potting soil. Then they should sprinkle a thin layer of sand over the soil. This will help students see any movement of soil.

Then, students prop up one end of the tray about 2 inches (5 cm). Have students predict what will happen when water is released over the higher end of the tray. One student should poke a hole with the tip of a pencil in the bottom of the paper cup. While holding a finger over the hole, the student should fill the cup with water, then release the water over the tray. All group members should record their observations.

Responding to Discovery

Discuss the results and have students propose what they could do to the soil to help keep the soil from washing away. Have them repeat the experiment with some rocks, leaves, and twigs mixed in the soil. They should record their observations.

Applications and Extensions

Ask students to look for evidence of erosion at home or at school.

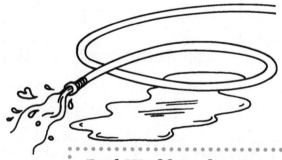

> **Real-World Applications**
> - mud slides
> - beach erosion

0-7682-3370-4 *Inquiry Science*

Soil Erosion

Draw the soil in the aluminum tray before and after adding water.

Before

After

Draw the soil with the changes you made. How did it look after you added water?

With Changes

Blowing in the Wind

Gearing Up

Retell or read "The Three Little Pigs." Discuss how the wolf was able to blow some of the houses over. Have students act like the wolf and try to blow a cotton ball, a crayon, and a stone. Discuss why some things could be blown and not others. Ask the students, "What is something that occurs in nature that is similar to blowing?" Discuss the effects of wind.

> ### *Process Skills Used*
>
> - observing
> - measuring
> - testing hypotheses

Guided Discovery

Background for the teacher:

Erosion is caused by natural forces. Weathering can be caused by wind, water, or temperature. Erosion can be modified by the use of the earth. Plants can stabilize the soil, while traffic can break it down more quickly.

Materials needed for each group:

sand

aluminum tray

a straw for each student

Directions for the discovery:

Students will fill the bottom of the aluminum tray with about a half inch (1–2 cm) of sand. Have student groups discuss what would happen if wind blew over the sand. Give each student a straw and, one by one, have them blow gently through the straw onto or over the sand. Tell students to blow softly so the sand does not leave the tray. Also, for safety, have all group members stand behind the blower. Smooth the sand between each student.

Responding to Discovery

Students should record their observations of the discovery, then propose changes to the sand that might help the sand "fight" against the wind. Students should test their proposals and record the results.

Applications and Extensions

Sing a new verse for the erosion song learned previously to the tune of "The Farmer in the Dell."

> The sand blows away,
> The sand blows away,
> Heigh ho, when strong winds blow,
> The sand blows away.

Challenge the students to make up a verse about stopping erosion.

> ### *Real-World Applications*
>
> - Learn about damage from sand and wind storms.
> - Desert rock formation

Name _____

Blowing in the Wind

Draw how the sand looked after someone blew on it.

What did you change? Draw the tray with your change.

What happened when you blew on the sand now?

 0-7682-3370-4 *Inquiry Science*

Dirt Is My Home

Gearing Up

Give students the opportunity to express what they know about animals that live in the soil. Give the students brown construction paper to draw a picture of one thing that lives in the soil. To create an underground look, students can spread glue over their pictures and sprinkle sand and soil over the glue. Have the class sit in a circle and sort and graph their animals.

Process Skills Used
- observing
- questioning

Guided Discovery

Background for the teacher:

Tiny organisms that may be barely visible to the naked eye can exist in soil. These may include bacteria, fungi, algae, and protozoa. Other, larger soil residents include earthworms, moles, badgers, and some insects and insect larvae.

Materials needed for each student:

rich soil sample with live critters (dug from a healthy garden)
magnifying glass
paper plate
worm to share (found in compost or at a bait shop)
clear jar for each group

Directions for the discovery:

Gently stir up the soil so any live critters are not all at the bottom. Give each student about a cup of the rich soil on a paper plate. Have students use a magnifier to examine the soil closely. Each student should draw a detailed picture of the soil sample on the activity sheet. They should look for evidence of living things (eggs, waste, decomposed organic matter, or live critters).

Give student pairs an earthworm to observe. Students should study the worms and think of questions they have about worms. Discuss student questions and help students find the answers.

Responding to Discovery

Have groups of students make a worm farm. Students can alternate layers of rich soil with layers of sand in a large, clear jar. The students can put the worms in the jar and cover the jar with a lid (containing holes). Students watch the worms over a week and observe what happens to the sand and soil layers. For an optimum environment, keep the soil moist, but not saturated. Store the jar in a dark area away from sunlight. You can add bits of ground-up food remains, such as apple peelings, egg shells, and other nonmeat foods (avoid acidic foods).

Applications and Extensions

Sing a song to the tune of "The Farmer in the Dell."

A worm lives in the soil,
A worm lives in the soil.

Oh look, the dirt's its home;
A worm lives in the soil.

Ask students to think of other animals to replace the worm in other verses.

Real-World Applications
- Learn about pests in a garden
- Worms are good for gardens.

Name _____

Dirt Is My Home

This is what I saw in the soil.

My worm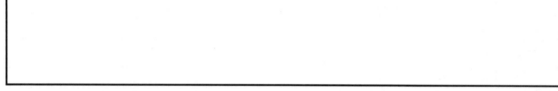

This is what happened
in our worm farm.

_____

_____

_____

_____

_____

_____

_____

_____

0-7682-3370-4 *Inquiry Science*

Performance-Based Assessment

3 = Exceeds expectations
2 = Consistently meets expectations
1 = Below expectations

Student Names

Lesson Investigation Discovery

Lesson 1: Geologist on the Go									
Lesson 2: Rock On!									
Lesson 3: Shake Rocks to Soil									
Lesson 4: Ice Rocks									
Lesson 5: Diggin' Dirt									
Lesson 6: What's in Soil?									
Lesson 7: The Scoop on Soil									
Lesson 8: Making Soil									
Lesson 9: Soil Soaking Test									
Lesson 10: The Heavy on Soil									
Lesson 11: Some Soil for Planting									
Lesson 12: Soil Erosion									
Lesson 13: Blowing in the Wind									
Lesson 14: The Dirt Is My Home									

Specific Lesson Skills

Can make reasonable predictions.									
Can make detailed observations.									
Can propose an explanation.									
Can follow directions.									
Displays curiosity.									
Can work cooperatively with a partner or group.									
Participates in discussions.									
Can complete a graph with data from investigations.									
Can classify data in meaningful categories.									
Can communicate through writing and/or drawing.									
Can apply what is learned to real-world situations.									

0-7682-3370-4 *Inquiry Science*

The Five Senses

0-7682-3370-4 *Inquiry Science*

Face Fun

Gearing Up

Engage students by playing the "I Spy" game. Students will gather in a central location. One student at a time will be given a pair of glasses. The student will spy something in the classroom ("I spy with my little eye something *green*.") and have the class guess the object.

Have students share what they know about their eyes and the sense of sight. Record their responses on a class chart.

> ### *Process Skills Used*
> - observing   • comparing
> - communicating

Guided Discovery

Background information for the teacher:
Our sense of sight orients us to our world and helps us interact with our environment.

Materials needed for each pair:
blindfold
yarn for hair
four sticky dots for eyes
crayon for drawing mouths
two buttons for noses
glue stick

Directions for the activity:
Pass out the student handout. Tell the students that they will be filling in the facial features while blindfolded. Explain which materials will be used for each feature. Before partners begin, they should predict how accurately they believe they will place each feature on the face outline. One student of each pair puts on the blindfold and is given page 67. The other student will hand each object to the student, one at a time. When all the facial features are placed, the students may remove the blindfolds and discuss with their partners the placement of

the features. Repeat with partners switching roles.

Responding to Discovery

Students will play the "look around" game to share what they have learned about the sense of sight. First, show the class a signal, such as raising your hand. Tell the students that you will be giving them a question to discuss with their partners. When they see you make the signal, they must stop discussing and copy the signal. Students will "look around" and see either the teacher or their classmates making the signal. Soon everyone will be quiet and ready to move on to the next question. Use the questions below or some of your own.

- Which of your five senses would have helped you complete the picture more accurately?
- Why was this difficult without your sight?
- What do your eyes help you do?
- What would you miss if you did not have your sense of sight?

Applications and Extensions

Have students create poems using the following format. Students should think about the things they love to see and include them in their poems. They may also illustrate their poems.

> I love to see
>
> _____, _____, _____,
> _____, _____
> with my eyes.

> ### *Real-World Applications*
> - How do blind persons make up for their lack of sight?
> - Play pin the tail on the donkey.

0-7682-3370-4 *Inquiry Science*

Face Fun

Glue the yarn for hair. Stick the dots in place for eyes. Draw a mouth with the crayon. Glue the button where the nose goes.

Describe the face you created.

_____

_____

_____

0-7682-3370-4 *Inquiry Science*

Peep Boxes

Gearing Up

Sing or recite "My Sight."

My sight, I see things dark and bright.
My sight, helps me see day and night.
My sight, shows me colors with light.
My sight, I see less color at night.
My sight.

Process Skills Used

- observing
- communicating
- proposing explanations

Guided Discovery

Background information for the teacher:
In order for a clear visual image to form, light rays must enter the eye. Without light, we cannot see objects. With reduced light, we may see things less clearly.

Preparation of Materials:
For each group of students, you will need three peep boxes. To make a peep box, poke a small peephole in the side of a shoebox. Cut a small ½-inch x 2-inch (1 cm x 5 cm) rectangular window on the cover of the box. Leave one side of the rectangle attached so the window can be closed to keep out light. Place a familiar object inside each box. Seal the cover with tape to keep out all light.

Directions for the activity:
The students will peek into each peep box with and without light. First, students will peek in the small peephole while covering the rectangular window with a hand or a piece of black paper. They should record what they think is in the box. Then, they may open the rectangular window and peek through the small peephole again. They should record what they think is in the box. Repeat for each box.

Responding to Discovery

Ask students to propose an explanation for why they could not see the object until they opened the window. Lead them to discover that light must be present in order to see an object.

- How does sight help you?
- What do your eyes need in order to see the object in the box?
- How far does the window have to be open before you can see the object?
- When could you see color in the box?

Applications and Extensions

Have students draw and color pictures in a dark room. Discuss how the pictures turned out. Did students make the same color choices they would make in the light?

Real-World Applications

- color blindness
- night lights
- Go outside at night and try to see color.

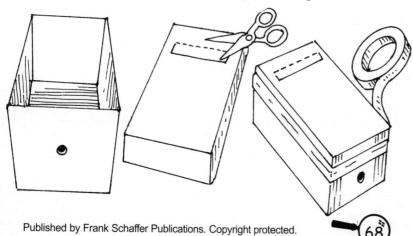

0-7682-3370-4 *Inquiry Science*

Name _____

Peep Boxes

What do you think you see in the box when there is . . .

Box 1

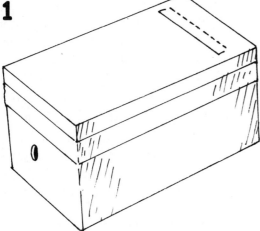

no light?

_____

light?

_____

Box 2

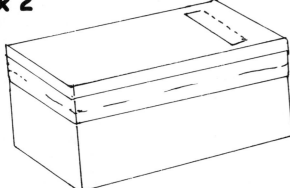

no light?

_____

light?

_____

Box 3

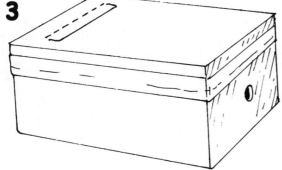

no light?

_____

light?

_____

Why do you think this happened? _____

_____

_____

0-7682-3370-4 *Inquiry Science*

Touch and Tell

Gearing Up

Expand students' vocabulary of words that describe textures. Send the students on a scavenger hunt in the classroom for a variety of textures. After 5–10 minutes, ask the students to meet in a circle and report what they have found. They should name the objects and describe their textures. Record the descriptive words on a chart.

Process Skills Used
- observing
- communicating
- comparing

Guided Discovery

Background information for the teacher:
Skin has thousands of receptors that detect texture, temperature, pressure, and pain. This activity will help students become more aware of their sense of touch.

Materials needed for each group:
Scraps or small quantities of the following: construction paper, glue, flour, corn meal, coffee grounds, glitter, colored sand, fabric swatches, aquarium gravel, paper towels, brown paper bag, other textured items that the students bring in

Directions for the activity:
Allow the students time to explore the different textures. They may sort them, describe them, and talk about where they have felt these before. Then ask the students to sort the textured items into categories and name the categories. On the recording sheet, ask students to write the names of their categories on the fingers. Below each finger, they should draw and label the items that fit in that category.

Responding to Discovery

Give each student several squares of heavy paper. (Cut index cards in half.) Tell them to glue small quantities or pieces of the textured items on the squares. Use the squares for sorting or matching games. Have the students label the squares. Help them with accurate spelling.

Discuss some of the following questions:

- What sense did you use in this activity?
- How did you sort the objects?
- How are the items alike and different?
- Did you use any of your other senses?

Applications and Extensions

Place the textured squares in paper bags (one per bag). Have the students identify and describe the texture or find a square with the same texture.

Students may continue to look for and bring in examples of texture.

Real-World Applications
- Display samples of Braille.
- What is the texture of pajamas and blankets? Why?

0-7682-3370-4 *Inquiry Science*

Name _____

Touch and Tell

Sort your different items according to touch. Write the categories on each fingertip. Draw and label the items that fit under each category.

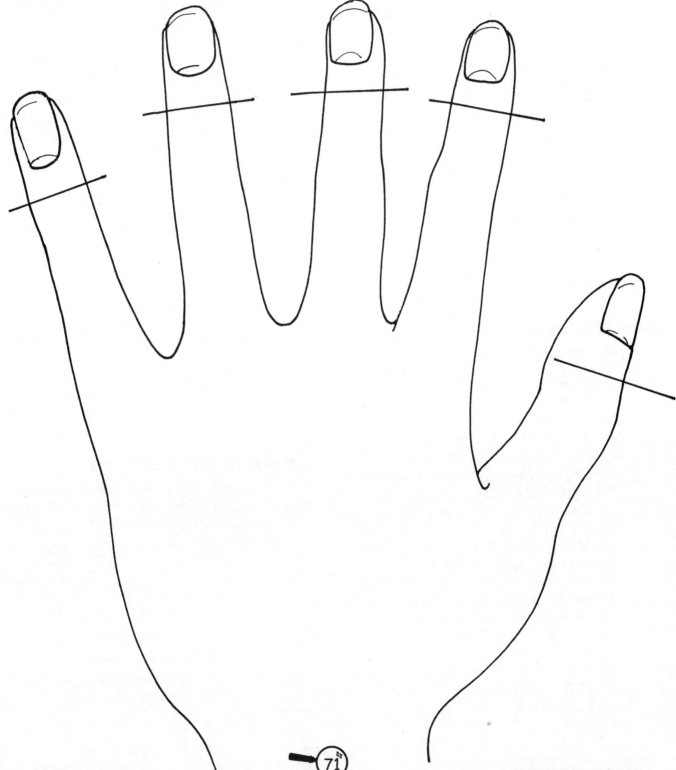

0-7682-3370-4 *Inquiry Science*

Feely Box

Gearing Up

Pair students up to play "match my cubes." The first student will secretly create a design with five Linking Cubes. He or she will hand the design to his or her partner under the table. The second person will use the sense of touch to recreate the object with five different Linking Cubes. Ask students to explain how they did it. What other sense might have been helpful?

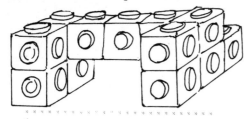

Process Skills Used
- observing
- predicting

Guided Discovery

Background information for the teacher:
Skin has thousands of receptors that detect information about the surrounding world.

Materials needed:
eight feely boxes (number each box)
items to place in the boxes:
    ping pong ball, miniature toy, Linking Cube, measuring cup, tennis ball, orange, plastic spoon, crayon

To make a feely box, cut a hole in a shoe box large enough for a hand to reach in. Cut the toes off an old, clean sock. Affix the sock around the outside of the hole and push the sock in the box.

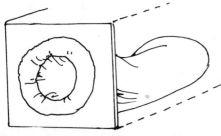

Directions for the activity:

Divide the class into no more than eight groups. Give each group a feely box. Students take turns feeling the object inside the box. Then, they write their predictions on page 73 by the correctly numbered box. When everyone has felt the object, they may pass the box to another group and receive the next box.

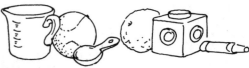

Responding to Discovery

Open each numbered box and show the students what was inside. Students can share what they had predicted was in the boxes. Discuss why they feel more confident about the object when they see it than when they feel it.

Discuss some of the following questions:

- When you were feeling the items in the boxes, what clues told you what the objects were?
- Would it have helped to have been able to smell the objects as well as feel them?
- Why do you think it is hard to identify an object using only the sense of touch?

Applications and Extensions

Have students work with partners to count sets of linked cubes using only the sense of touch. Partners can verify the correct number of cubes.

Real-World Applications
- How would you learn about math if you could not see?

0-7682-3370-4 *Inquiry Science*

Name _____

Feely Box

Feel the object inside each box. Write your predictions beside the numbered boxes below.

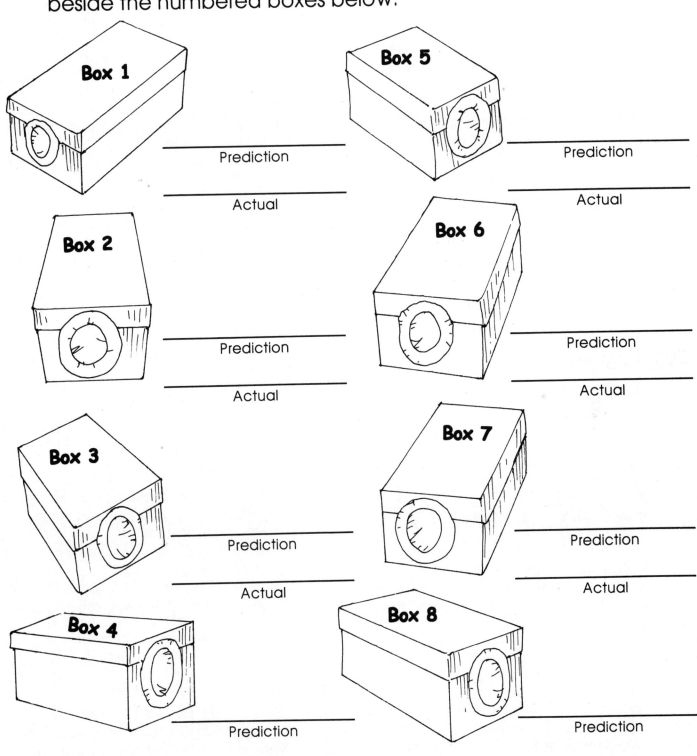

Box 1

_____
Prediction

_____
Actual

Box 2

_____
Prediction

_____
Actual

Box 3

_____
Prediction

_____
Actual

Box 4

_____
Prediction

_____
Actual

Box 5

_____
Prediction

_____
Actual

Box 6

_____
Prediction

_____
Actual

Box 7

_____
Prediction

_____
Actual

Box 8

_____
Prediction

_____
Actual

0-7682-3370-4 *Inquiry Science*

Sensing Connections

Gearing Up

Gather and display several different types of balls (ping pong, basketball, whiffle, softball, soccer, foam, plastic, rubber, golf, tennis, baseball, etc.). Ask a volunteer to sort the balls without telling how they were sorted. Discuss with the class how they think the balls were sorted. Ask another volunteer to sort them differently. Continue until there does not seem to be any other way to sort the balls.

Discuss how the different balls are used. Discuss the senses used when playing each game.

> ### Process Skills Used
> - observing
> - predicting
> - making a model

Guided Discovery

Background information for the teacher:
Students will use their sense of hearing and the sense of touch to play a game.

Materials needed for each group of three students:
a round balloon
a small bell to tie to the balloon
a blindfold

Directions for the activity:
Show the student a balloon that is blown up with a bell attached to the stem. (You may prepare the balloons for each group ahead of time.) Demonstrate how to play a game in which you roll the balloon back and forth across the floor with a partner. In groups of three, students prepare their balloons and practice rolling it to each other. Stop the groups and ask each student to record a prediction on page 75 of how many times

out of ten he or she will be able to catch and return the balloon while blindfolded.

One student in the group will be blindfolded at a time. The blindfolded member will sit across from another member and play the game. The third member will assist in recovering the balloon and keeping count of the number of times the balloon is rolled by the blindfolded person out of ten tries.

After the ten rolls, the blindfolded member removes the blindfold and records the actual number of successful catches and returns. Group members switch roles until each member has been blindfolded.

Responding to Discovery

Hold a discussion in a large circle. The teacher asks a discussion question and rolls the balloon to someone in the circle. That person answers the question or starts the discussion and rolls the balloon to someone else who adds to the discussion.

Discuss some of the following questions:
- When you rolled the balloon, what senses did you use?
- Was it easy to catch and roll the balloon while wearing the blindfold?
- How would the game change without the bell attached to the balloon?
- When is it helpful to feel things even though you can see them?
- How might a blind person play ball?

Applications and Extensions

Challenge the students to invent a new ball game that you must play blindfolded. Encourage the use of a different sense.

0-7682-3370-4 *Inquiry Science*

Sensing Connections

Record your prediction before you play. How many times out of ten can you catch and return the balloon? Graph your prediction and actual counts.

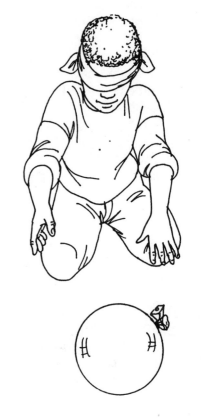

	Prediction	Actual
10		
9		
8		
7		
6		
5		
4		
3		
2		
1		

Were you surprised by your results? Explain.

_____

_____

_____

_____

0-7682-3370-4 *Inquiry Science*

Pattern Block Problem

Gearing Up

Draw the following pattern on the board and have the students act it out with you.

jump, jump, skip, clap, jump, jump, skip, clap, jump, etc.

When students are comfortable with the pattern, keep the pattern but change the actions (clap, clap, snap, wink). Then ask the students to rename the pattern, such as "triangle, triangle, square, X." Finally, assign the pattern letters (AABC). Try the same sequence with other patterns. Allow the students to propose patterns.

> ### Process Skills Used
> - observing
> - patterning

Guided Discovery

Background information for the teacher:
Students will use their sense of touch to recreate patterns. They will use their sense of sight to confirm their patterns.

Materials needed:
pattern blocks
poster putty
tagboard strips
shoeboxes with holes cut for hands
    to reach in on both sides

Directions for the activity:
Ask students to use pattern blocks to recreate letter patterns that you write on the board (ABBCC, ABBA, ABAC, ABAB, etc.). Each student should choose a favorite pattern and attach it to a tagboard strip with poster putty.

Place one pattern block pattern under each overturned shoebox. Have students reach in and feel the blocks without looking. Then have students try to recreate the patterns with pattern blocks. When they are finished, lift the boxes and compare.

Responding to Discovery

Discuss some of the following questions:

- How did your pattern compare to the one in the box?
- What senses did you use in this activity?
- What makes something a pattern?
- Where else do you see or feel patterns?

Applications and Extensions

Put up a small wall between two students to hide their workspaces as they work on the floor. The wall may be an open folder standing upright. One student will construct a simple design with pattern blocks. Using verbal directions, the builder will explain his or her design to a partner who will try to construct the same design with pattern blocks. The partner may ask questions to clarify directions. Remove the wall to compare completed designs.

> ### Real-World Applications
> - finding patterns
> - comparing
> - communicating

0-7682-3370-4 *Inquiry Science*

Pattern Block Problem

☙ Draw the pattern you felt and created.

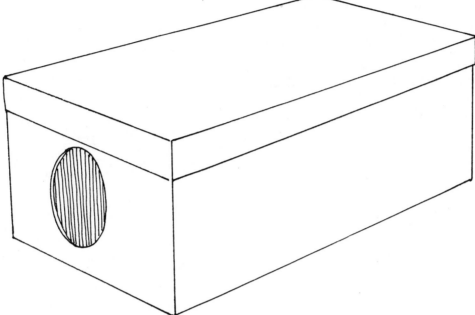

☙ Draw the pattern you saw inside the box.

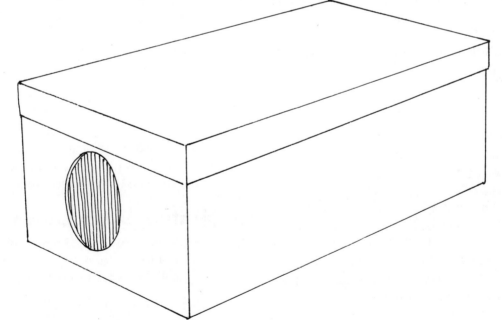

☙ What did you discover?

_____

_____

Tasty Treats

Gearing Up

Show students a mystery bag with a secret food item inside. Tell them they may ask yes or no questions to guess the mystery object.

Brainstorm a word web about our sense of taste. Ask students to name any words they think of that relate to taste. Post the word web on the wall. Add to the web as more words come up.

> ### Process Skills Used
> - observing
> - comparing
> - controlling variables

Guided Discovery

Background information for the teacher:
Students will use their sense of taste. The tongue can sense the taste of foods through tiny receptors called taste buds. Information about taste also comes from the odor of foods.

Materials needed:
paper plates
2–4 peeled and cubed potatoes
2–4 peeled and cubed apples

Directions for the activity:
Tell the students that they will be tasting food items without the help of their senses of smell, sight, or touch. Students will work with a partner. Make sure all children wash their hands before handling food.

Student A of each pair should close his or her eyes and hold his or her nose. Student B of each pair should place a cube of apple or potato on student A's tongue. Student A should guess which food it was. Repeat with the second food chunk. Then reverse roles.

After both partners have tasted and guessed the food, partners may taste the apple and potato with all their senses.

Responding to Discovery

Use the "walk, freeze, talk" method to engage students in a discussion. All students stand and begin to walk around the room. The teacher calls out "freeze," and students stop and find a close partner. The teacher poses a question for the partners to discuss. Discuss some of the following questions:

- Was it easy to identify the foods when you couldn't see or smell?
- Did the foods look alike?
- When you could see and smell the food, how did the taste change?
- What other sense works with your sense of taste to give information about food?

Applications and Extensions

Try the same experiment with eyes closed but allow students to use their sense of smell. How are the results different?

> ### Real-World Applications
> - nutrition
> - cooking and favorite foods
> - taste testing

0-7682-3370-4 *Inquiry Science*

Tasty Treats

Close your eyes and hold your nose. Taste the first chunk of food. What is it? Circle your guess.

 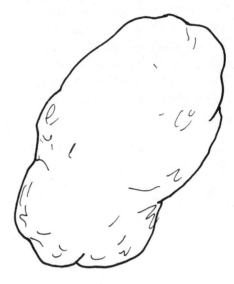

Taste the second chunk of food. What is it? Circle your guess.

Taste the apple and potato again with all your senses. How did the taste change?

_____

_____

_____

0-7682-3370-4 *Inquiry Science*

Tickle Your Tongue

Gearing Up

One by one, give the students samples of foods from the four taste categories (lemonade, candy, potato chips, and unsweetened cocoa). After each taste, ask students to describe the taste. Lead the students to identify the four major tastes that the tongue can sense (bitter, sweet, sour, salty).

> ### Process Skills Used
> - observing
> - predicting
> - collecting data
> - graphing

Guided Discovery

Background information for the teacher:
Taste buds are grouped on the tongue on the front of the tongue, on the sides, and on the back of the tongue. Taste buds are also found in other parts of the mouth.

Materials needed:
lemonade
small cups
bitter chocolate powder
candy
toothpicks
small mirror

Directions for the activity:
Have students observe their tongues with small mirrors. On page 81, students draw and color the details on their tongues. Give each student a toothpick and one or more samples of the foods tasted in the introduction. Challenge the students to locate groups of taste buds on their tongues. They should dip the toothpick in the food and touch the toothpick to their tongues in

various places, testing where the flavors are strongest. When they locate taste buds, they can label them on the drawings of their tongues.

Responding to Discovery

Discuss some of the following questions:
- Where on your tongue were the flavors strongest?
- Which taste did you like the best?
- What are your favorite foods?
- Why doesn't everybody like the same foods?

Applications and Extensions

Make a class graph of students' favorite foods. Discuss the data on the graph.

Poll other students in the school about their favorite foods. Can you find any patterns of food preferences by grade level or gender?

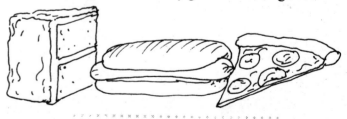

> ### Real-World Applications
> - nutrition
> - favorite foods
> - taste testing

0-7682-3370-4 *Inquiry Science*

Name _____

Tickle Your Tongue

🔊 Add details to the tongue to show what your tongue looks like.

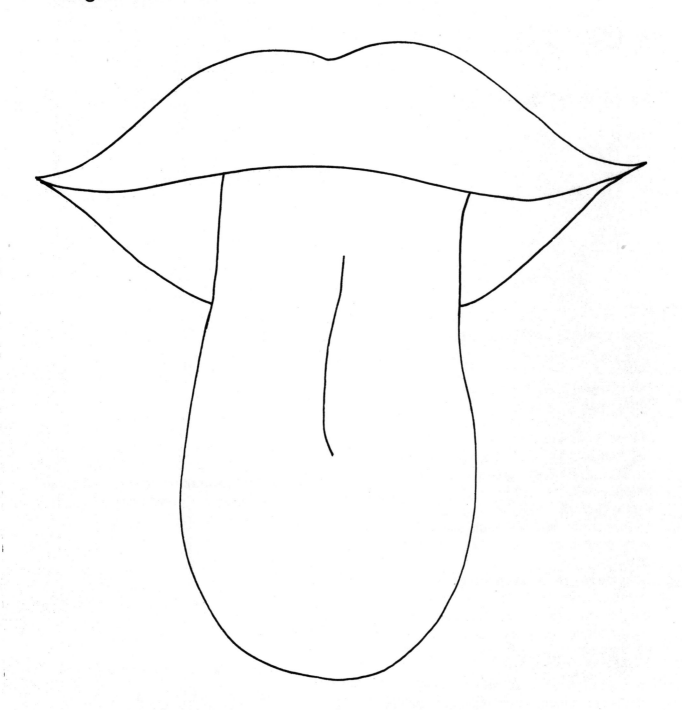

🔊 Label the taste buds.

0-7682-3370-4 *Inquiry Science*

Matching Smells

Gearing Up

Ask all the students to close their eyes while you spray some perfume into the air. Tell them you want them to use one of their senses to observe the thing you just brought into the room. Ask them to identify which sense they used to observe it. Brainstorm a list of smells and have the students categorize the words as good smells or bad smells. You may need a Venn diagram for this.

Process Skills Used
- observing
- comparing
- communicating

Guided Discovery

Background information for the teacher:
We can smell things when molecules of a substance are carried into the nose with an intake of air. The molecules stimulate the olfactory nerves, which send messages to the brain. Taste and smell are completely separate senses, but we usually smell and taste at the same time.

Materials needed:
film canisters with pinholes in the top
    (enough for half the class)
cotton balls
Scented items to put in the film canisters
    (use cotton balls for liquid scents):

rubbing alcohol	vinegar
vanilla extract	lemon oil
peppermint	coffee grounds
onions	perfume
soap pieces	cinnamon
peanut butter	chocolate
banana chunk	juice

Directions for the activity:
Put a scented item or scented cotton ball in each film canister. On index cards, write the names of the items found in each canister.

Read the cards with the students so they know what smells they are trying to identify. Pass out the canisters to half the class and the cards to the other half. Without speaking, students must walk around smelling canisters and reading cards. The object is to find a person holding the smell that matches the card or the card that matches the smell. The game can be played several times by passing out the canisters and cards to different students.

Responding to Discovery

Have students complete page 83.

Discuss some of the following questions:
- Was it easy to identify smells without seeing the smelly object?
- What other senses might have helped you in this activity?

Applications and Extensions

Play "What's my smell?" Write the good and bad smells from the brainstormed list on individual index cards. Without allowing the students to see their own card, tape a card to each student's back. Students may ask other students questions about the smell. The object is for each student to identify the smell on his or her own back. When all students have guessed their smells, the game is over.

Real-World Applications
- Discuss other food smells.
- Can you identify what's cooking or baking from the smell?

Matching Smells

~ What smells did you smell in the film canisters? _____

_____

_____

~ Draw and label some pleasant and unpleasant smells.

Pleasant	Unpleasant

0-7682-3370-4 *Inquiry Science*

The Nose Knows

Gearing Up

Stand in the front of the room and place a jar with something smelly in it on a table in front of you. Have the class stand facing you in a line in the back of the classroom. Read the following poem to the class.

I like to smell roses and hot apple pie,
I like to smell Daddy all dressed in a tie.
My nose helps me smell lots of things near
and far.
I wonder can you guess the smell in the jar
. . . from where you are?

If none of the students can identify the smell, let them move one step closer until someone can.

> ### Process Skills Used
> - observing
> - measuring
> - collecting data

Guided Discovery

Materials needed:
paper plates
measuring tapes
rulers
moth balls
perfume
coffee grounds
peppermint extract

Directions for the activity:
Keep all of the different smelly items in sealed containers until it is time to use them. Place one of the items on a paper plate. Allow students to creep (several may approach at once from different directions) toward the plate and signal at the point when they can smell the scent. They may put a piece of masking tape and initial that spot. Then, each student should measure the

distance from the scented item to where he or she first smelled it. Test each of the items in the same manner. Students should record their measurements on page 85.

Responding to Discovery

Have students graph their measurements from page 85. Then, discuss their observations about their graphs. Did everyone agree about which items they smelled first and last? Discuss why some items might be smellier than others.

Provide smelly markers for students to color a smelly picture.

Applications and Extensions

Investigate the amount of time that students smell a new scent. Do they continue to smell it over a period of time? Is the scent fading or do they get used to it? Can students smell themselves?

> ### Real-World Applications
> - Can you smell your own breath?
> - What are some familiar smells at home?

0-7682-3370-4 *Inquiry Science*

Name _____

The Nose Knows

Item smelled	Distance to item	The smell was . . .	
		Strong	Weak

Observations: _____

_____

_____

_____

0-7682-3370-4 *Inquiry Science*

Simply Sounds

Gearing Up

Play the telephone game and surprise the students about how easily sounds are mistaken for other sounds. Students should sit in a circle. Whisper the following sentence in one student's ear: "Pink and purple penguins went on a picnic." That student whispers the same sentence in his or her neighbor's ear. In this manner, the sentence should be passed to every student. The last student should say the sentence aloud. Compare the final sentence with the original and each sentence the students heard along the way. Ask students to hypothesize about why the sentence changed so much.

> ### Process Skills Used
> - observing
> - inferring
> - comparing

Guided Discovery

Background information for the teacher:
Our ears help us hear. The outer ear is shaped like a funnel to catch sounds and channel them to the inner ear. The receptors for hearing are located in the inner ear. They send signals to the brain, and the brain interprets the sounds.

Materials needed for each group:
4 shoeboxes
penny   key
marble   crayon

Directions for the activity:
Before class, number the shoeboxes from 1–4. Place one item in each box. Place the penny in each number 1 box. Place the marble in each number 2 box. Place the crayon in each number 3 box. Place the key in each number 4 box. Seal the boxes with tape. Give the four boxes to each group.

The students will infer what is in each box by observing how the object sounds and feels as they move and shake each box. They should record their guesses in the numbered boxes on page 87. When everyone is done, open the boxes.

Responding to Discovery

Discuss what made the objects in the boxes easy to identify and what made them difficult to identify. Would it have helped to know ahead of time what the four objects were without knowing which boxes they were in?

Sing "I Hear."
(to the tune of "The Wheels on the Bus")

I hear the popcorn go pop, pop, pop,
Pop, pop, pop . . . pop, pop, pop.
I hear the popcorn go pop, pop, pop,
On the kitchen stove.

Add other verses with familiar sounds, such as the thunder goes boom, the kettle goes hiss, and the dog goes woof.

Applications and Extensions

Create a paper megaphone or paper cup telephone. Explore the way sound travels.

> ### Real-World Applications
> - discerning instruments in music
> - recognizing voices on the phone

0-7682-3370-4 Inquiry Science

Simply Sounds

๛ Draw what you think is in each box.

1. Actual _____	**2.** Actual _____
3. Actual _____	**4.** Actual _____

0-7682-3370-4 *Inquiry Science*

Sound All Around

Gearing Up

Play "Who's Talking." Have students spread out all over the classroom and sit down. Tell the students to close their eyes while you tap someone. That student should stand up and say a sentence (you may provide a sentence in advance). The class may open their eyes and guess who spoke. You may play the game several times. Discuss what made the game easy or difficult.

Process Skills Used
- observing
- inferring

Guided Discovery

Background information for the teacher:
Sounds coming from the sides are easily identified. Sounds from the front and rear and overhead are more difficult to locate. Having two ears improves hearing.

Materials needed for each group:
blindfold   bell or other signal

Directions for the activity:
Divide the class into groups of five. Tell the class that they will be conducting an experiment to find the location and direction of sound. One student from each group will sit in a chair with a blindfold on. A different student in the group rings the bell or makes a sound. The blindfolded person points in the direction from which he or she believes the sound is coming. A different member of the group should help the blindfolded person record on page **89** the origin of the sound and where the student pointed. Allow each student several opportunities to listen and point.

Responding to Discovery

Discuss from which direction were most students able to identify the sound. Discuss ways they could make it easier to hear and locate sounds. Try out any reasonable proposals.

Have students design a paper megaphone or an ear trumpet. Have students try it out. Does the trumpet help them locate the origin of the sound? Discuss.

Applications and Extensions

Have the students close their eyes and put their heads down. Ask them to listen quietly for several minutes and keep track of what sounds they hear. After the time is up, brainstorm a list. Sort the list in ways that students suggest (quiet sounds, sounds we usually don't notice, loud sounds, familiar sounds, etc.).

Real-World Applications
- What is the purpose of foghorns?

0-7682-3370-4 *Inquiry Science*

Name _____

Sound All Around

Draw a musical note showing from where you think the sound came. Draw an **X** where the sound actually occurred.

Watch your classmates try to point to the sound. What did you notice?

_____

_____

0-7682-3370-4 *Inquiry Science*

Sensing Connections II

Gearing Up

Have the students stand in line. Tell them that you will test how fast the class reacts. The last person in the line will have a timer. That person will start the timer and tap the person ahead of him or her in line. When that person feels the tap, he or she will tap the person ahead of him or her in line. The taps will continue one at a time up the line until the first person in line is tapped. That person says stop, and the timer stops and announces the time. After this practice run, students will predict their best time in three trials. Record all predictions on the chalkboard and test it.

Process Skills Used
- observing
- recording data

Guided Discovery

Background information for the teacher:
Our perceptions of the world around us are mainly built around our senses of sight and sound.

Materials needed for each pair:
ruler
a blindfold

Directions for the activity:
This activity will explore reaction time first with the sense of hearing, then with the sense of sight.

One student will drop a ruler vertically (with the 1 inch mark on top) between the fingers of his or her partner's open hand. The partner will try to close the hand in time to grab the ruler. In the first trials, the grabbing partner will be blindfolded. The dropper will let the grabber know the ruler has been dropped by making a clicking sound. Read the measurement where the thumb or index finger caught the ruler. Record the measurement on page 91. Repeat three times.

Remove the blindfold and try to catch the ruler, this time with the sense of sight returned. The dropper should not make the clicking sound this time. Record three trials. Compare the results.

The students should switch roles.

Responding to Discovery

Discuss the following questions with the students using the "Number-Off" strategy. Students sit in groups of four. They number off from one to four in each group. The teacher will pose a question for the groups to discuss. They discuss the question. Then the teacher picks a number from one to four and that student will share the results of the discussion with the rest of the class.

Discuss one of the following questions:

Was it easier to catch the ruler using your sense of sight or sound?

What other sense did you need in this activity?

Did your reaction time improve with practice?

Applications and Extensions

Have students continue to investigate their reaction times by developing a relay course on the playground. Students move around obstacles and run the course in the least amount of time. Give students the opportunity to practice and then time each child.

0-7682-3370-4 *Inquiry Science*

Name _____

Sensing Connections II

🐌 Record where you caught the ruler each time while wearing a blindfold. Number each trial.

🐌 Remove the blindfold and repeat. Record where you caught the ruler each time.

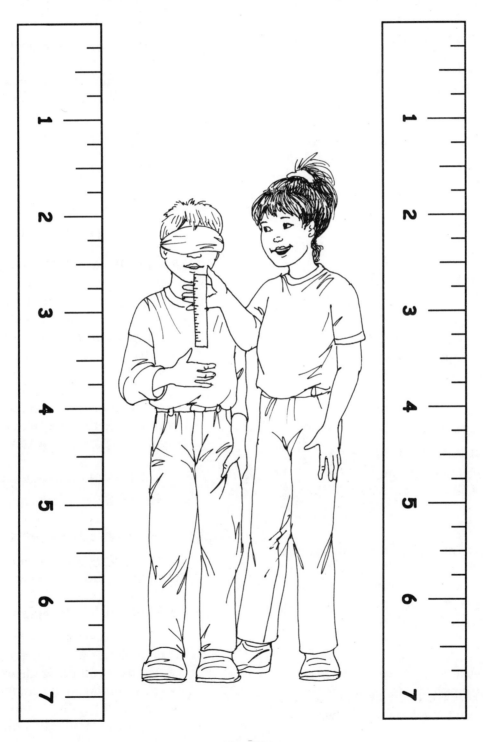

0-7682-3370-4 *Inquiry Science*

Sensible Situations

Gearing Up

Begin the lesson with this poem about the five senses.

We each have five senses that we use every day.
We observe our big world as we go on our way.

We each have a tongue that tastes what we eat,
Foods that are bitter, salty, sour, and sweet.

And we each have two eyes that look all around
At stars in the sky or the grass on the ground.

We each have a nose that smells good and bad.
Do you like the cologne worn by my dad?

I have two ears on the sides of my head.
I hear lots of sounds and the things that you said.

We're covered with skin from our heads to our toes.
It feels a soft puppy or the prick of a rose.

Process Skills Used
- observing
- classifying
- communicating

Guided Discovery

Background information for the teacher:
We have senses that provide us with information about the world. The senses may warn us of danger (hot) or provide a feeling of pleasure (good smell). Some senses require contact such as touch or taste. Other senses may pick up information from a distance. We actually have other senses, such as sense of heat, pain, hunger, thirst, and fatigue.

Materials needed:
oranges broken into sections
paper cups
paper towels

Directions for the activity:
Give each student a few sections of orange in a paper cup. The students will make observations of the oranges using the five senses and record the observations on page 93. Guide the students to make the observations in the following order: sight, touch, hearing, smell, and taste.

Responding to Discovery

Set up five tables in the classroom and label them with the five senses. Set up the number of chairs you would like at each table. There should be more chairs than students so they have some, but not unlimited, choice. Ask students to think about which sense they would like to discuss. Then allow them to move to that table—they may have to go to a second choice. At each table, the students should discuss what made them choose that sense and brainstorm a list of good things about that sense. They should choose one person to report their list to the rest of the class.

Have the members of the groups create artwork for a five senses bulletin board.

Applications and Extensions

Go on a senses walk. When you return, discuss the students' observations.

Real-World Applications
- How do your senses affect your safety?
- How do you sense danger?
- Discuss personal tastes.

0-7682-3370-4 *Inquiry Science*

Name _____

Sensible Situations

🐦 Use your five senses to make observations about the orange.

1. I saw . . .

2. I felt . . .

5. I tasted . . .

3. I heard . . .

4. I smelled . . .

0-7682-3370-4 *Inquiry Science*

Performance-Based Assessment

3 = Exceeds expectations
2 = Consistently meets expectations
1 = Below expectations

Lesson Investigation Discovery	Student Names									
Lesson 1: Face Fun										
Lesson 2: Peep Boxes										
Lesson 3: Touch and Tell										
Lesson 4: Feely Box										
Lesson 5: Sensing Connections										
Lesson 6: Pattern Block Problem										
Lesson 7: Tasty Treats										
Lesson 8: Tickle Your Tongue										
Lesson 9: Matching Smells										
Lesson 10: The Nose Knows										
Lesson 11: Simply Sounds										
Lesson 12: Sound Alll Around										
Lesson 13: Sensing Connections II										
Lesson 14: Sensible Situations										

Specific Lesson Skills										
Can make reasonable predictions.										
Can make detailed observations.										
Can propose an explanation.										
Can follow directions.										
Displays curiosity.										
Can work cooperatively with a partner or group.										
Participates in discussions.										
Can complete a graph with data from investigations.										
Can classify data in meaningful categories.										
Can communicate through writing and/or drawing.										
Can apply what is learned to real-world situations.										

0-7682-3370-4 *Inquiry Science*

0-7682-3370-4 *Inquiry Science*

0-7682-3370-4 *Inquiry Science*